AFTERSHOCK

AFTERSHOCK

HELP, HOPE, and HEALING
IN THE WAKE of SUICIDE

DAVID COX & CANDY ARRINGTON

BROADMAN
&HOLMAN
PUBLISHERS

Nashville, Tennessee

0–8054–2622–1

Published by Broadman & Holman Publishers
Nashville, Tennessee

Dewey Decimal Classification: 155.9
Subject Heading: SUICIDE \ DEATH \ GRIEF

Contact the authors for speaking engagements
or seminars by calling

864-579-7202
E-mail AFTERSHOCKHHH@aol.com

or mail to
2375 East Main Street
Suite A–105
Spartanburg, SC 29307

1 2 3 4 5 6 7 8 9 10   10 09 08 07 06 05 04

Dedicated

To my dad,
John Woodbury Cox,
loving Christian husband and father,
Sunday school teacher and deacon,
active in community service,
decorated World War II and Korean War veteran,
lover of trains and baseball,
and
a victim of suicide.

—David

To my dad,
Hugh Asbury Neely,
loving Christian husband and father,
Sunday school teacher and deacon,
decorated World War II veteran,
builder of solid houses,
strong family ties,
loving relationships,
and
a victim of cancer.

Thank you for teaching me I can do all things through Christ.

—Candy

Contents

Preface   ix

Acknowledgments   xi

1. Suicide: An Earthquake of Catastrophic Proportions   1

2. Interpreting Fault Lines: The Suicidal Mind   11

3. Distant Tremors: Depression and Teen Suicide   28

4. Surveying the Devastation: The Survivors   51

5. Bent but Not Destroyed: Beyond the Family Scars   66

6. Picking Up the Pieces: Deciding to Rebuild   83

7. Understanding Seismic Indicators: Suicide Intervention   99

8. Restoration: Double Joy   110

Endnotes   130

Preface

In a casual conversation, David mentioned to Candy, "I've always wanted to write a book, but I don't have any idea how to go about it."

"I've never written a book before, but I know what to do," Candy responded.

Several work sessions produced a proposal, outline, and sample chapter. The foundation was laid. The words of Psalm 127:1 became the theme for the project: "Unless the LORD builds the house, they labor in vain who build it" (NKJV).

Candy met Len Goss of Broadman & Holman at the 2001 Blue Ridge Mountain Christian Writer's Conference. She presented the proposal to him, and was surprised when six other conferees spontaneously shared their personal stories of suicide's impact on their lives. Len said, "I thought your idea was too narrow, but now I see this table is a microcosm of society. There *is* a need for this book."

Although this book is coauthored, for the ease of the reader it is written in first person with David as the speaker, except where noted. Candy researched, conducted interviews, and prepared the manuscript. David offered insights from his personal experience with suicide, his paramedic career, and his counseling ministry. The project was very much a joint effort, and neither could have produced the book without the other.

The book is written specifically to survivors of suicide—those left behind following a suicide—but will also be helpful to ministers, those in intervention, and anyone who struggles with what to say to those who have experienced a devastating life crisis. The sections on depression, fear, and forgiveness are applicable to anyone, not just to people dealing with suicide. Our heartfelt prayer is that the message of this book will bind wounds and open a pathway of hope and restoration to the grieving.

The Lord's hand has been on this project from its inception. We acknowledge his direction and leadership in all phases of the writing and publishing process. God has done, and continues to do, amazing things. This book is nothing about our abilities, but everything about God at work in us. To him be all the glory.

Acknowledgements

With special thanks from David:

- To my wife, Kelly, for reflecting Jesus with your life.

- To my children—Scott, Phil, Kellyn, Leslie Ann, and Luci—for the opportunity to be to you what my dad was unable to be to me.

- To my coauthor, Candy, for challenging me and encouraging me to write this book. It wouldn't exist if it were not for you.

- To my mother, Lunelle Comer, for holding our family together after the earthquake.

- To my wonderful sisters and fellow survivors, Nancy and Janet.

- To my pastors, Don Horton and Tony Cribb, for all the years of support and encouragement.

- To Kirk H. Neely, my mentor, who first saw the counselor in me.

- To Phil Phillips, Sunday school teacher, basketball coach, big brother, and friend.

- To the Spartanburg S.O.S. group, where I first saw the need for this book.

- To my loyal and trusting counselees, for giving me the opportunity to minister.

With special thanks from Candy:

- To my husband, Jim, for your love, encouragement, support, and editing skills. I love you and am thankful for our life together.

- To my children, Neely and Jay. I love you both with all my heart.

- To David, my coauthor and friend, for allowing me to "build this house" with you. You are the brother I never had.

- To my mother, Mildred Neely, my most ardent cheerleader.

- To the survivors, for sharing their stories.

- To Linda Gilden and Dalene Parker, for manuscript review and comments.

- To Len Goss, who caught the vision and took a chance on two virtually unpublished authors.

CHAPTER 1

❧

Suicide:
An Earthquake of Catastrophic Proportions

"But God intended it for good to accomplish what is now being done, the saving of many lives" (Gen. 50:20).

DAVID'S STORY

On July 17, 1967, an earthquake rocked my world. Felt by relatively few people, it devastated those of us at its epicenter and brought chaos to our lives. Although not a dynamic force of nature, the event shook my universe, crumbled my stable foundation, and sent shockwaves far into the future. It was suicide.

Suicide is a subject I would rather consign to a dusty corner of my mind. I would like to but can't because I think about it every day. Whether in my counseling ministry or in the shadowy haze of memory, suicide is a topic I cannot escape.

In a nine-year-old boy's mind, life in Memphis, Tennessee, was perfect. Then July 17 dawned. On that day my perfect world was shattered; my life was forever changed.

I was cutting the grass when I saw my father pull out of the driveway in his white 1966 Mustang. To this day, when I see one of those cars, an involuntary shudder hits me, yet I keep a die-cast model of his car on my desk to remind me that God causes all things to work together for good (Rom. 8:28). As usual, I shouted out over the roar of the mower, "Dad, where are you going?" I expected to hear his familiar reply, "Goin' crazy. Wanna come along?"

That day the answer was different. "I have to go somewhere." His answer puzzled me. He drove off, than stopped the car to look back at me. The look on his face will forever trouble me. If only I had known what he was going to do, the "somewhere" he was going, could I have said something to stop him? I've relived that moment a million times. I never saw him alive again.

My mother found his note when she got home. She was frantic, but I didn't know why. She sent me off to the neighbor's house while she contacted the police. I spent a sleepless night there, separated from my family, wondering, as I peered out the window, why all those police cars and people surrounded our house. I later learned the police found his body at the horse show arena during the night. Why my father chose that location for his death is still a mystery to me.

The next day I had a sense of urgency about going home. I tried to enter the house, but it felt almost as if I were crossing a picket line. Arms reached out to intercept me, and I was prevented from going inside. This was when my concern increased, and I became fearful that something had happened to my mother. Up to this point, I never associated Dad's odd behavior the previous afternoon and my mother's sense of panic with the ensuing chaos at our house. Later, after being taken to a house I had never been to before, I was brought home. People jammed the room. My mom was lying on the couch. Although I was relieved to see her, I knew something was very wrong. My mother was alive, but she seemed incapacitated. Because she couldn't tell me herself, my Sunday school teacher broke the news of my father's death to me.

My mother waited until the night before the funeral to tell me that my father had killed himself. I remember sitting on the end of her bed while she told me. I guess she delayed a day or so because she was trying to shield me or didn't know how to tell me. Certainly, we were all living in a state of shock. Telling me must have been one of the hardest things she ever did in her life. Finding out the truth after everyone else knew was one of my first sources of anger. My father's obituary read "self-inflicted gunshot wound." It was in print for everyone to see. Today an obituary would never say that.

We actually had two funerals, which was very hard. Following the service in Memphis, we immediately left for South Carolina where my mother's family lived. Despite double funerals, I never grieved the loss. I stayed in South Carolina with relatives, whom I knew loved me—but whom I had seen only occasionally—while my mother and sisters returned to Tennessee to sell the house and tie up loose ends.

Remaining in South Carolina kept me separated from the ordeal, but this didn't stop me from feeling disconnected and displaced. Almost immediately, I wished I had returned to Memphis with my family. I was very homesick and kept thinking, *Who am I going to lose next?* My mother's cancer surgery several years earlier played at the fringes of my mind. The possibility that she might be the next to die worried me.

Life changed dramatically after that. The move to South Carolina meant leaving a nice middle-income home for a small rental house. Ties with friends, some personal belongings, and all things familiar were broken. The decision to move was made independent of me. From an entry in my sister's diary, I believe my mother and sisters made the decision the day after my father's body was discovered.

It was a logical decision because my mother's family was in South Carolina, but I wanted to move back to North Carolina to the home-town I remembered. There life seemed normal: *before* my mom's ill-ness, *before* my oldest sister went away to college, and *before* my dad began trying to outrun the depression that was overwhelming him. We moved three times in two years. I was searching for stability. Now there seemed to be no chance of that.

As with the move, no one discussed my father's death with me, signaling the shame I felt was accurate. I wondered if my South Carolina relatives even knew my father had killed himself. Since no one talked about him, I assumed they didn't know the circumstances of his death.

Not until I enrolled in a new school (the fourth school in four years in four different states) six weeks after his death did the impact of my father's suicide become real to me. As I filled out paperwork on the first day, I saw the blank that said, "Father's Occupation." Then it hit me. Shame, anger, guilt, betrayal, rejection, and loss cascaded over me like debris falling from an earthquake-ravaged building. I wanted to escape but couldn't. There was nowhere I could go to get away from the churning emotions I was experiencing.

I was the last one to see my father alive. That was both a gift and curse. It felt strangely special to be the final family member to see him just before his death. But also, somewhere deep inside, I felt I was responsible because perhaps he saw me as his last hope for rescue, but I missed his cry for help.

In retrospect, I can see it was impossible for a nine-year-old to pick up on the warning signals. It is not unusual for loved ones to blame themselves, no matter how unreasonable their sense of responsibility.

The fact that I was the last one to see my father alive made it much harder to understand the delay in telling me that he was dead and had killed himself. If my dad wanted me to be the last to see him alive, shouldn't I be among the first to know the truth? I kept wondering if I had information others didn't have about my dad that might have saved him. If I had been consulted earlier, would my input have made a difference?

During the next few years, I hardly spoke of my father at all for fear of someone asking me where he was or how he died. If they did ask, my answer was, "He had 'heart problems.'" This answer, although a lie, was not totally false. His heart, "sick" from loss of hope, ultimately led to his death.

Talking about the circumstances of his death was unacceptable. At a time when our family should have clung together for strength and support, we struggled silently with our own private pain. I realize now there must have been a lot of late-night telephone calls between my mother and sisters, but I never knew about them.

The family makeup in the home went from five to two almost overnight. Both of my sisters were in college, so I was alone with my mom. I didn't know what to say or do, and neither did she. I can remember on several occasions pretending I didn't know my father had committed suicide in an attempt to get her to tell me the story all over again. She never took the bait, or perhaps she thought I had blocked out the circumstances of his death and didn't want to tell me. To this day, thirty-six years later, my mother and I rarely speak of my father's death.

Even as a child, I could tell my mother was sad. I took her picture once about six months after Dad's death. She was looking out the window and had the saddest expression on her face. I know she must have been thinking about him. I still have a hard time looking at that picture because it reminds me of those long-ago emotions.

By the age of thirteen, my feelings of anger and guilt were so great I was almost dysfunctional. I missed fifty-four days of the seventh grade, locked in my room, sleeping and watching TV. Probably the only reason I passed was because I did well the days I was present and was not a behavior problem. But I was mad at my father for taking the coward's way out and killing himself. At the time, I don't think I equated my emotional problems with Dad's suicide.

To go along with my anger was an overwhelming sense of guilt for being angry with a parent I longed to have alive and present in my life. I remember composing suicide notes as a teenager although I never followed through with a gesture or attempt. I took out a lot of my anger on my mom, something I regretted later. I guess she was just an easy target. Now, as an adult, I realize she did a wonderful job getting all of us through this awful period.

Although I don't think my mother saw the connection between my anger and the suicide, she took me to a psychologist for counseling. Many times parents are caught off guard by the lag time children experience between the event and the manifestation of anger and depression. Since a period of years has passed, they assume the child's problems are not related to an earlier trauma.

Outwardly, I was annoyed by being forced to go to a "shrink." Inwardly, I was terrified the doctor or my mother thought there was something wrong with me. *Maybe I was crazy, too!* Now, when I counsel teenagers, I try to remember how I felt. I let them know in the first session that I understand their reluctance about coming to counseling.

As a teen, I hated going to the sessions, although I met with the psychologist only about four times. They were mostly unproductive in dealing with the root of my anger and fear of abandonment because, as far as I can remember, we never discussed anything about my father or his death, although I may have blocked that out. The psychologist gave me several different kinds of tests. The most vivid memory I have of this is working puzzles. *How dumb is this?* I remember thinking. At some point, I began to wonder if the psychologist even knew how my father had died. Surely my mother told him, but he never mentioned it. I got the message loud and clear that suicide was something you didn't discuss.

Not until seven years after my father's death was I able to tell anyone he had killed himself. I was sixteen years old and attending a camp. Following a skit that hinted at suicide, a girl dissolved into tears and ran outside. I overheard someone say she was so upset because her brother had recently committed suicide. Because I identified with her pain, I felt I should approach her and tell her about my dad. It was the first time I had spoken of it to anyone.

While still at camp, it bothered me that I had told this girl my secret. Had I betrayed others by this? She wanted to stay with me constantly. I was uncomfortable with that, not because I didn't like her but because it made me think about everything again. Her clinginess reminded me of how emotionally unhealthy I probably still was and had been immediately after Dad's death. I felt almost smothered by her (more my issue than hers). This experience caused me to withdraw even further from divulging my story to anyone, unless I absolutely had to. Later, I was able to understand from this experience how important it is for survivors to have someone they can identify with and talk to. Not talking is probably one of the most destructive things for a survivor.

I could hardly wait for the camp to be over so I could get home. I think I wanted to distance myself from the girl I had confided in. I wasn't ready to help anyone else yet. Also, I was dating someone at home and felt I had betrayed her by telling another person first. It seemed important to get home and make things right. It took me a while to work up the courage to tell my girlfriend, and when I did, she just accepted it as information. This huge thing in my life that I was telling only for the second time was basically no big deal to her, or so it felt. I'm not sure what reaction I was looking for, but she simply said, "Oh."

During the next few years, the only other person I told was a college friend whose mother tried to commit suicide. He talked to me about his experience, and afterwards I told him about my dad. I convinced myself I was handling things because I was able to tell those three people over an eleven-year period of time.

Then, as a seminary student, I went to a campus film festival and saw Alfred Hitchcock's *Frenzy.* In the surprise twist at the end of the movie, the villain appeared to be about to shoot someone. At the last minute, he turned the gun around facing straight at the camera, as if turning it toward himself, and fired. The whole place erupted into applause and cheers, and something inside me snapped. Here was this whole room full of people cheering and clapping because someone had just committed suicide!

I fell apart emotionally. I was mad and upset and kept thinking how insensitive everyone was. I had to get up and leave. It was then I realized I had a lot of work to do to come to terms with my father's suicide and that I probably needed some help doing it.

I started going to counseling sessions while still in seminary and continued with counseling while in a chaplaincy program. It was during the chaplaincy counseling that I was able to begin to work through things. During this time, I worked in the emergency room and the psychiatric unit and saw many completed suicides and suicide attempts. This was very hard at first, but eventually these units were where I wanted to be all the time. I was determined to stare suicide down and not run from it.

Even after the counseling, telling my future wife about the skeleton of suicide was one of the most difficult things I ever did. I delayed telling my own children about the circumstances of their grandfather's death as long as possible and then only because they were going to hear me discuss it on the radio talk show where I was promoting a suicide survivor's support group. At the last minute, I realized I had to tell my children. They didn't need to hear it over the radio.

But I couldn't do it. The bondage of shame surrounding my father's death still had a choke hold on me. I asked my wife to take the responsibility of telling our children. It was just something I didn't want to face. I remember thinking, *How ironic, I'm promoting a survivors' group, yet I can't even tell my own children.*

For years, I thought my father's situation was unique. Now I see it was not. Because there was much shame associated with his death, my personal journey toward healing and peace was long and circuitous. Had I chosen to allow it, the disgrace and anger surrounding my father's death might have rendered me useless or ineffective in God's kingdom. My father's suicide could have forced me to a level of withdrawal where ministering to others would have been impossible. But I feel this event in my life has enabled me to counsel with the degree of compassion and understanding necessary to reach hurting individuals.

My clinical pastoral education supervisor, Todd Walter, told me something once that helped me immensely. He said, "You'll get to a place where you can talk about your father's suicide openly, but it will never be without a wince of pain in your soul." That is exactly the way it is today.

Although I cannot bring my father back, because of the circumstances of his death I have discovered I have the capacity to minister to suicidal persons and their families. I didn't choose for suicide to be part of my history. But I praise God that the good that came from my father's death is greater than the harm. I am grateful my dad didn't decide to "take" my mother, sisters, or me with him. So often suicide victims also commit homicide, thinking it spares those who remain the shame of surviving.

Only within the past five years have I reached the point where I can say that I wouldn't change the fact that my father committed suicide, even if I could. There are days when I doubt the truthfulness of this statement, but I trust God to continue to perfect the work he is doing in and through my life. My prayer is that I will always be a willing servant in the saving of many lives.

Like the Old Testament character, Joseph, I identify with his painful journey into bondage. I also experienced abandonment, loneliness, fear, and anger. Joseph, abandoned by the brothers he trusted, was separated from his beloved father. Given the choice, I would never have chosen to be separated from my father. Joseph went from life in a big family to a life of slavery and loneliness in unfamiliar surroundings. I moved to an unfamiliar town with only my mother.

When Joseph's brothers came to Egypt to ask for help during a famine, Joseph displayed a wide range of emotions. Even though the actions of his brothers were in the past, Joseph remained angry, accusatory, and difficult. When he saw his younger brother Benjamin for the first time, he was overcome with emotion to the point of having to leave the room for a time. I have also experienced all these emotions and flashbacks of emotional pain over the years. It hasn't kept me from functioning, but I've had to work around and through the emotions.

Even today, it is still very painful for me to relive the events surrounding my father's death. The pain is not a "paralyzing pain" but something like the pain from hard exercise—stretching, purging, cleansing, purifying. There is a part of me that wants to believe it is all a bad dream. I keep hoping that I will wake up at the neighbor's house across the street where I spent that long, awful night, that the nightmare will be over, and my father will be alive.

Like Joseph, I have come to a place of victory. God blessed him and caused him to find favor in the land of his captivity. God's hand was on his life even though Joseph was in a difficult situation. The same is true for me.

Looking at all of this again in writing this book has been much harder than I anticipated. Many feelings have surfaced, some that I haven't felt in more than thirty years, some for the first time. Perhaps I still have some work to do. The healing process is ongoing. Only those who have experienced the pain of suicide can understand how it lingers and ebbs and flows. But you can reach the point of living victoriously. I have!

"And we know that in all things God works for the good of those who love him, who have been called according to his purpose" (Rom. 8:28).

AFTERGLOW

1. What is your story? You may find it helpful to write about the death of your loved one. In a separate journal or notebook, chronicle your own personal encounter with suicide. Use as much detail as possible. Include the circumstances surrounding the death and your thoughts and feelings before and after. Although this exercise may be extremely painful, it will help you accept the reality of the death and begin to deal with your loss.

2. If it has been years since your loved one's suicide and your memories are fragmented, revisit the place where you were living at the time. Go to the church where the funeral took place, other places of significance, look at newspaper articles and pictures of your loved one. Allow yourself to remember.

CHAPTER 2

⁂

Interpreting Fault Lines:
The Suicidal Mind

"Hope deferred makes the heart sick" (Prov. 13:12).

The quake starts with a low rumble. At first, it is impossible to tell if you really felt something or just imagined it. Everything around seems normal. The tremor, which briefly shook the room, can surely be explained away as a sonic boom or road construction. There is really nothing to be concerned about.

Many times the family and friends of a suicidal person are living in a quake-prone area without realizing it. Often the victim has been emitting undetected seismic activity for months, but those around have denied, ignored, or not felt the rumblings.

Prior to an earthquake, evidence of fault lines exists either on the surface or underground. Active faults, though not moving for decades, can move many feet in a matter of seconds, producing an earthquake. The final rupture will probably begin along one of these cracks as the strain becomes great enough to spread.

Just as geologists often misinterpret faults on the earth's surface, so warning signs in suicidal persons are often overlooked. Sometimes neither the victim nor his loved ones are aware the warning signs indicate a deeper problem. Just as scientists cannot see deep inside the earth to determine exactly what is happening before an earthquake, those around a suicidal person cannot fathom the level of anguish being experienced before the final event.

DISPELLING THE MYTHS ABOUT SUICIDE
"My people are destroyed from lack of knowledge" (Hos. 4:6).

Suicide is a subject shrouded in mystery and myth. In fact, the actual word *suicide* is not used in the Bible. Many Christians approach suicide with a confusing variety of opinions because the Bible gives us little information on the subject, other than recording several instances of people who took their own lives. There are seven completed suicides recorded in Scripture:

1. Abimilech (Judg. 9:52–55)
2. Samson (Judg. 16:28–30)
3. Saul (1 Sam. 31:3–6)
4. Saul's armor-bearer (1 Sam. 31:3–6)
5. Ahithophel (2 Sam. 17:23)
6. Zimri (1 Kings 16:18–19)
7. Judas Iscariot (Matt. 27:3–5). The account of Judas' suicide is the only reference to suicide in the New Testament.

Although the deaths of Abimilech, Zimri, Ahithophel, and Judas could be interpreted as God's punishment for sin, each made the decision to end his own life.

Saul apparently committed suicide to avoid disgrace and potential physical atrocities at the hands of his captors. There is no indication in Scripture that Saul's suicide was viewed with disapproval, because he was given a war hero's burial. Saul's armor-bearer is a perfect example of suicidal tendencies in survivors. Whether the result of fear or grief, or both, the armor-bearer followed Saul's example and took his own life.

While Samson died by his own hand and his last words in Judges 16:30 were "let me die with the Philistines," his death is not always included in a list of suicides in the Bible. Many consider his death not to be a suicide but a last heroic act of vengeance on his enemies.

Although the morality of suicide is not directly addressed in the Bible, we are given commands and principles that speak to the issue. Surely, the command "You shall not murder" (Exod. 20:13) must apply since suicide is self-murder. The Bible says that we will be held accountable for our actions and will answer to God for them. It never says we will be eternally damned for committing suicide or any other sin against the body. In 1 Corinthians 6:19–20 we read, "You are not your own; you were bought at a price. Therefore honor God with your body." There is nothing about suicide that honors God.

My father was a Christian, a deacon in his church, and a Sunday school teacher, but none of those things kept him from taking his own life. He made the choice. I feel certain that when my father was ushered into the presence of God, he was asked to give account for his actions by his heavenly Father. Taking the path of least resistance by choosing to end his life rather than trusting God to see him through his difficulties certainly represents a lack of faith on his part. But I do not believe he is spending eternity in hell.

It appears that the early church fathers used a mixture of pagan and Jewish tradition to formulate their views about suicide. Jews living at the time of Christ saw suicide as a heinous sin. Josephus wrote that the body of a suicide victim should not be buried until after sunset and then without normal funeral rites. The Jews even questioned Jesus' potential for suicide as evidenced in John 8:21–22, "Once more Jesus said to them, 'I am going away, and you will look for me, and you will die in your sin. Where I go, you cannot come.' This made the Jews ask, 'Will he kill himself?' Is that why he says, 'Where I go, you cannot come'?"

The Catholic Church tried to stop people from committing suicide by declaring it an unpardonable sin. During the medieval period, proper Christian burial was denied those who committed suicide, and relatives and friends were discouraged from accepting suicidal bequests. In his writings, Dante placed those committing suicide in the seventh circle of the inferno.

Thomas Aquinas, a prominent opponent of suicide in the Middle Ages, believed a person who killed himself was excluded from being granted absolution for the sin of suicide, and therefore had committed a mortal sin. In his *Summa Theologica,* he objected to suicide as a violation of *natural* law, which prescribes self-love; *moral* law, because suicide is an injury to the community; and *divine* law, because it violates the sixth commandment.

In some ways, the church's stand has been shaped by society's attitude toward suicide. With society's ever-changing attitude on the subject, including the present trend toward euthanasia as a means of coping with terminal illness and aging, it is easy to see why Christians have such a broad range of opinions. Many Christians object to suicide, but they have difficulty justifying their objection with biblical evidence. Others are adamant that a person who commits suicide, whether Christian or not, goes straight to hell. Some hold the opinion that suicide is proof the person was never really saved in the first place. Nowhere in Scripture is this idea substantiated. Salvation does not stop a person from sinning. We still sin even after salvation. Suicide is a sin like any other, and it does not indicate a lack or loss of salvation.

Although some segments of the body of Christ feel suicide is a sin for which there is no forgiveness, I do not see anything in Scripture to support this. Certainly, suicide is a sin, but there are many other sins. Scripture tells us that the only unpardonable sin is blasphemy against the Holy Spirit (Matt. 12:31). John Calvin concluded that suicide should not necessarily be viewed as blasphemy. Suicide does not invalidate the covenant of salvation God established with the person through a personal relationship with Jesus Christ.

Modern society struggles with a number of other myths and misunderstandings about suicide in addition to the question of suicide as an unpardonable sin. Take the following true/false quiz to determine if your current ideas about suicide are based on fact or myth.

1. Suicide accounts for relatively few deaths in the United States.   T_____ F_____
2. Talking about suicide will plant the idea in a depressed person's mind.   T_____ F_____
3. People who talk about suicide usually don't follow through with it.   T_____ F_____
4. Most suicides occur without warning.   T_____ F_____
5. The tendency toward suicide is inherited.   T_____ F_____
6. If there is no suicide note, it was not a suicide.   T_____ F_____

7. When depression lifts, suicide is no longer
a concern.   T____ F____

8. A suicidal person cannot be talked out of
it if he is intent on dying.   T____ F____

9. Women threaten suicide, but only men
follow through with it.   T____ F____

10. Only certain people are the suicidal type.   T____ F____

11. Only insane or "crazy" people commit
suicide.   T____ F____

12. People who commit suicide haven't sought
medical help before the attempt.   T____ F____

THE ANSWERS AND THE FACTS

1. **Suicide accounts for relatively few deaths in the United States (False).** Every seventeen minutes, someone in the United States commits suicide. Each day approximately eighty-six Americans commit suicide, and fifteen hundred people attempt suicide. Suicide is the nation's eighth leading cause of death. For those fifteen to twenty-four years of age, suicide is the third leading cause of death. More Americans, an estimated 31,000, kill themselves than are killed by homicide. For every completed suicide, there are twenty-five attempted suicides. An estimated 750,000 suicide attempts annually affect the lives of millions of family members. The number of survivors grows by 186,000 each year. For every suicide, the lives of at least six other people are affected.

2. **Talking about suicide will plant the idea in a depressed person's mind (False).** This is not an accurate assumption because a depressed person has usually considered suicide long before it is mentioned by someone else. This myth is one that costs more lives than it saves. A suicidal individual is actually relieved that someone has finally noticed his pain. Talking about suicide decreases the troubled person's vulnerability by reducing his isolation. A person isolated in his pain is much more likely to commit suicide.

3. **People who talk about suicide usually don't follow through with it (False).** Suicidal people really want help more than they want

to die. Talking about killing themselves is a cry for help. Many people through fear and ignorance do not acknowledge this cry for help and refuse to get involved. When I worked as a paramedic and was called to the home of a suicide, the family was always shocked. But as they talked, I usually heard something to the effect of "he always said he was going to kill himself, but we didn't know he was serious about it." You can be sure that when a person talks about suicide, he or she is seriously considering it.

4. **Most suicides occur without warning (False).** It may seem a suicide has occurred without warning, but usually some sort of suicidal gesture has taken place before the act. Any of the following are clues to a suicidal mind-set: withdrawal, moodiness, depression, aggression or risk-taking, alcohol and drug abuse, eating disorders, personality changes, threats, giving away possessions, and diminished sexual interest. Although it may appear to the family that the event was without warning, usually a psychological autopsy of the suicide victim reveals suicidal warnings.

5. **The tendency toward suicide is inherited (False).** There is no genetic predisposition to suicide. But suicides do tend to run in families. Suicide has a negative affect on surviving family members, which sometimes leads to suicidal thoughts or attempts on their part. Suicidal behavioral patterns do seem to follow family lines.

6. **If there is no suicide note, it was not a suicide (False).** Approximately two-thirds of those who commit suicide do not leave a note.

7. **When depression lifts, suicide is no longer a concern (False).** When a depressed person experiences a period of apparent improvement, his overall condition may actually be one of greater danger. Improvement may be a result of resolving to go ahead with suicide and relief that the struggle of making the decision is over.

8. **A suicidal person cannot be talked out of it if he is intent on dying (False).** Almost every suicidal person is struggling with the decision to live or die. There are usually two internal voices shouting yes and no. All it may take to save a life is for a concerned family member or friend to step in and show interest in the suicidal person's struggle. For a person wavering between choosing life or death, a con-

cerned, compassionate, external voice can tip the scales to the side of choosing to live.

However, there are some situations where no matter how hard an intervener tries, the person is past the point of no return.

9. Women threaten suicide, but only men follow through with it (False). Although women make far more suicidal gestures than men, they attempt suicide less often than men but usually choose slower-acting, less-lethal methods, such as prescription medications, thus increasing their chance of rescue and survival.

Men make far more suicide attempts. Suicidal behavior in men seems to be more lethal. Men complete suicide about three times more effectively than women because they are more likely to use faster-acting, more lethal means, such as guns or cars. This probably explains why more men actually commit suicide. Men try harder.

10. Only certain people are the suicidal type (False). Although some people are at higher risk of committing suicide, there is no suicidal personality type. Suicide tends to be a cross-cultural phenomenon affecting all socioeconomic groups.

11. Only insane or "crazy" people commit suicide (False). A person who thinks about or tries to commit suicide is not necessarily insane. It is possible for negative thought patterns and depression to overtake anyone to the point of wanting to end it all. If someone in your family committed suicide, this doesn't make that person or you crazy. Sadly, this stigma is still attached to many surviving families in our society.

12. People who commit suicide haven't sought medical help before the attempt (False). Many times physical ailments accompany depression. Suicidal people often seek medical treatment for physical problems before an attempt. Some seek counseling but get discouraged when they don't see immediate results and discontinue counseling.

ᦏ ᦏ ᦏ

Suicide doesn't happen suddenly, although it may appear to. The suicidal mind-set builds over a period of time as a progression of negative thoughts take place. Hopelessness and helplessness are the hallmarks of suicidal thought. Other common emotions in people who attempt suicide are pain and loneliness.

There is often a predisposition toward suicide before the act occurs. There is a difference between a suicidal gesture and a suicide attempt. Before a person in crisis makes a genuine suicide attempt, he will generally make suicidal gestures. A gesture is an early cry for help and often comes in the form of verbal clues: "I'll just end it all." "You won't be seeing me around here any more." "No one needs me." A suicidal gesture may also come in the form of taking an overdose of medicine, self-mutilation, reckless driving, or purchasing or handling a gun. Suicide attempts as opposed to suicidal gestures are more lethal and usually occur after other means of getting help have failed.

The person's intent may be to wave a red flag not actually kill himself. Suicidal gestures usually increase in severity until the cry for help is heard. Sadly, suicidal gestures are often unsuccessful in getting needs met and may lead to a suicide attempt or even an accidental suicide. The goal was not actually to end life but to seek some escape from pain.

Unintended suicide happens when a person is not completely sold out to the idea of dying; he simply uses too lethal a means to cry for help. All suicidal persons are seeking a way out of their pain. It is not death they are seeking; it is an end to the pain.

Frequently, substance abuse plays a role in depression and suicidal thought. Sometimes a suicidal person will use drugs or alcohol to get up the courage to commit the act. Substance abuse may be intended to dull the pain of a depressed individual, but this ultimately intensifies the depth of the pit in which he finds himself. As David stated in Psalm 31:9–10, life becomes a hopeless place: "Be merciful to me, O LORD, for I am in distress; my eyes grow weak with sorrow, my soul and my body with grief. My life is consumed by anguish and my years by groaning; my strength fails because of my affliction, and my bones grow weak."

&% &% &%

Seismologists believe earthquakes can never be accurately predicted because they are unpredictable. Such may be the case with those contemplating suicide. Although some suicidal people talk about what they are planning, many remain mysteriously silent.

Teenagers are especially adept at concealing their thoughts and intentions before attempting suicide. They are more capable than adults of carrying on a normal routine while struggling with depression and suicidal thoughts.

When the quake finally hits, the person completes the act so long contemplated. For the suicide victim, the end has come. For those left behind, the devastation has just begun.

I still remember clearly where I was and what I was doing the day my father took his own life. He was forty-eight when he decided self-inflicted death was preferable to life. My father experienced a classic midlife crisis precipitated by a number of circumstances, including my mother's cancer surgery, the expenses of two daughters in college, several job changes within two years, an unsold house, health problems, and deep financial debt. In the face of all this, he saw nothing in his future that provided even a ray of hope.

Although there is no way to truly understand the mind of a suicidal person, the best way to come close is to imagine a life totally devoid of hope. Hopelessness is the universal thread running through all suicidal thought.

When hope is lost, even if circumstances improve, the person may be past the point of no return. As a heart attack is often fatal, this is a "heart attack" of a different kind. Proverbs 13:12 states, "Hope deferred makes the heart sick." The writer is referring not to the physical heart but to the soul—the place where hope resides. Once all hope is gone, it is possible that no amount of intervention can turn the situation around.

Over the years since my father's death, I have struggled to understand why his problems were so great in his mind that death seemed to be the only way out. From correspondence and his suicide note, it is obvious that an unsold house from a previous move was probably his greatest source of anguish. In a letter to the real estate agent dated a week before his death, he stated, "The house *must* be sold." In his suicide note, he said, "I have been *so* depressed about the house."

On the day my father killed himself, he sent me out to get the mail. Among the day's mail was a letter from the real estate agent saying she had a sales contract on the house. For years it has bothered me that this letter was not sufficient to stop my father from killing himself. Why wasn't it enough? It was an answer to what appeared to be his greatest concern, yet he followed through with the act of killing himself.

His suicide note was dated several days before his death. I feel his mind was already set on following through with his decision, so much so that the news of the impending sale of the house was not enough to change his mind. I have come to the conclusion that he felt his last act of usefulness for his family was to provide for us financially by his death.

Suicide has often been described as a permanent solution to a temporary problem. When life's problems, whether real or imagined, are so overwhelming that a person sees no light at the end of the long, dark tunnel around him, putting an end to that life seems to be a sensible solution. A suicidal person's anxiety level is immeasurable. It is difficult for someone who has never experienced that level of anxiety to understand its effect.

Many factors may exist in the life of a person who is contemplating suicide. Usually a combination of events or issues that seem irreconcilable is involved. Often the person feels there is no one who cares enough to be interested in his problems, or he doesn't want to burden anyone with his distress. When a person has no network of support, when there is no one to talk to, the pressure and stress continue to build. If the person has no way of letting off some steam, eventually the tension becomes so great that suicide begins to seem like a viable option.

Depression is always at the root of suicide. I have never counseled a suicidal person who was not depressed. Depression stems from two of the most basic human emotions: fear and anger. Fear leads to anger. Generally, the reason a person manifests anger is because of fear that a need will go unmet. Anger leads to depression. Depression is best described as anger turned inward. As this pattern progresses, depression turns to thoughts of suicide.

Unresolved conflict, divorce, debilitating debt, personal illness or the illness of a loved one, relationship problems, job stress or loss of a job, and any other out-of-control circumstances can lead to depression and potentially suicidal thoughts. Men are especially susceptible because they often do not have strong peer relationships and tend to isolate themselves. When the emotions surrounding life's stresses are held inside and not expressed, fear and anger boil beneath the surface.

Depression is a common problem that can affect people of all ages. The symptoms include: inability to think clearly or concentrate, change in appetite, weight gain or weight loss; irritability or agitation; an inability to carry out normal responsibilities; feelings of worth- lessness, guilt, or low self-esteem; overwhelming sadness; uncontrolled crying; sleep disturbances; and physical problems such as fatigue, headaches, backaches, nausea, or indigestion. For a person living under the effects of depression, suicidal thought is often within easy reach.

Just as rock formations shift and slide along a fault line, so is life full of transitions. When physical, emotional, or financial problems enter the equation of these life events, people often become overwhelmed. A suicidal person probably feels he is the only one who has ever gone through the life crisis he is suffering. When coping skills are not in place and help is not sought, fear and anger churn like molten rock in the center of the person's life, and the pressure becomes overwhelming.

For a person living under the influence of depression, hopelessness, and helplessness, the pressure builds over a period of time. Just as heat and pressure build under the earth's surface before an earthquake, so a suicidal person feels the rumblings of something uncontrollable deep within. The pain and frustration intensify until suicide seems to be the only avenue to peace.

LARRY'S STORY

Recall scenes from the movie *Coal Miner's Daughter,* and you can picture the small, mountainous, eastern Kentucky coal-mining town where Larry grew up. The town is so remote it is forty miles to the nearest hospital. Larry describes the residents of his hometown as "good people but hurting people." His father and most of his family were miners. With a low education level and little hope of escaping the monotony and depression of work in the coal mines, suicide has been a continual problem in the community. The average suicide statistics for a county this size are 5 per 100,000. For Larry's region they are 16 per 100,000.

The eighth of nine children, Larry remembers the first funeral he attended, the first person he ever saw in a casket, being a suicide victim. It is ironic that Larry works today as a funeral director.

Tragically, Larry's family and extended family history is riddled with suicide attempts and completions. His father contracted black lung and was forced to take disability. This led to self-esteem problems coupled with already existing emotional problems. Larry describes his father as a critical person. Although he is quick to add, "There was never a time I didn't love my dad." He also says his father made friends easily and was well thought of in the community.

When Larry was thirteen years old, his brother closest in age to him attempted suicide. Their parents were having marital problems, and the brother experienced conflicts with their father. Larry was at home alone with his brother. His brother told him he was going to move out and go live with a sister and her husband because of the conflict in the home. His brother instructed him to take care of their mother, went to another part of the house, and took a whole bottle of prescription pain medication.

Larry was waiting for a ride to a church function when his mother came home. His brother was still coherent enough to tell her what he had done. When Larry's ride arrived, they immediately took his brother to the hospital. He lived. Larry experienced guilt later because he didn't pick up on his brother's hints about suicide. Another brother also attempted suicide with a drug overdose.

A sister attempted suicide while going through a divorce. The prospect of raising two children as a single parent in a community that didn't offer much hope of a second marriage or career opportunities led her to depression and a suicide attempt. Her attempt, also a drug overdose, failed. Years later, her second husband successfully completed suicide by shooting himself.

In the late 1980s when Larry's father had been on disability almost twenty years and was confined to the house on oxygen, he attempted suicide twice with drug overdoses. Suffering from other health problems and failed surgeries, in addition to black lung, his father was addicted to pain medication and sleeping pills. As his father saw himself declining physically, his emotional and mental problems escalated. Larry said there was great fear in his family during this time that his father would commit a murder-suicide, killing their mother and himself. "As my father slowed down, he had more time to think," Larry said. "He realized what he was becoming. I believe he thought he was doing his family a favor by trying to kill himself."

While visiting his dad in the hospital following the second attempt, Larry's father promised him he wouldn't try again. "The good Lord must want me here for some reason," he said. But two of Larry's uncles committed suicide that year, and he feels this "encouraged" his father to try again. One of the uncles took his own life just three weeks before Larry's father's completed attempt. Years of living with physical problems, depression, suicidal thoughts, and examples took its toll. "My father's death didn't come as a shock to me even though he promised me he wouldn't attempt suicide again," Larry said.

In a discussion with one of his brothers following their father's death, the brother stated he felt suicide was "their destiny." Larry determined to make it otherwise. While still living in Kentucky, he formed his first suicide survivors' group. "I did it to help me face the problems within my family. Perhaps I am a little too open about telling that my father killed himself, but it helps me deal with the shame. If I tell people up front that I have a suicide history, I don't have anything to hide."

He started a second group while working in Tennessee, then was instrumental in starting the Survivors of Suicide (S.O.S.) group in Spartanburg, South Carolina. After talking to Dr. Cox (coauthor of this book), meeting with a representative from the Mental Health Association, and gaining financial support from a local mortuary, the group met for the first time in March 1997. Through local media coverage and distribution of brochures about the group through mortuaries, cemeteries, hospitals, rescue units, and churches, the initial group met with twelve to fifteen people present. Although members have come and gone, the group remains a place of healing and encouragement for those who are grieving a suicide loss.

When asked if he has ever felt suicidal, Larry says he's taken steps to make sure he doesn't succumb to the family legacy. "It's too big a decision to leave to chance. I've made an agreement with myself that if I ever do feel like I'm headed in that direction I'll get help. Getting out of the area where I was raised has helped. I guess I will always have anxiety and be very concerned about my brother and sisters and their state of mind. With our history, it's hard not to have suicide on my mind."

&8 &8 &8

Living Short of Victory

One of the most heartbreaking parts of my ministry is seeing Christians who live their lives as if they have no hope. I estimate 90 percent of my suicidal counselees are Christians; yet being followers of Christ does not make them immune to suicidal thoughts. In fact, in some ways Christians who have suicidal tendencies live in a greater state of despair. They want to view suicide as an option, but they have too much guilt because of their religious convictions to actually attempt suicide. This guilt adds to their anxiety and compounds their suicidal mind-set. If anything, Christians seem even more prone to satanic attack and suicidal thought patterns than non-Christians.

The apostle Paul describes these people in 1 Corinthians 3:1–3 as worldly Christians. Although these people belong to Christ, Paul speaks to them not as spiritual people, but as babes in Christ. In verse 3, he tells us that these lives are marked with envy, strife, and divisions. They are not living with the power and victory Christ intended for them. Sadly, this may be the most miserable of all conditions. These people are looking forward to the hope of heaven, but their relationship to Christ doesn't make their situation any less desperate.

Even Paul, who could hardly be described as a carnal Christian, may have experienced one or more suicidal crises. In 2 Corinthians 1:8–10, Paul declared, "We do not want you to be ignorant, brethren, of our trouble which came to us in Asia: that we were burdened beyond measure, above strength, so that we despaired even of life. Yes, we had the sentence of death in ourselves, that we should not trust in ourselves but in God who raises the dead, who delivered us from so great a death, and does deliver us; in whom we trust that He will still deliver us" (NKJV).

In Philippians 1:21–25, Paul said, "For to me, to live is Christ, and to die is gain. But if I live on in the flesh, this will mean fruit from my labor; yet what I shall choose I cannot tell. For I am hardpressed between the two, having a desire to depart and be with Christ, which is far better. Nevertheless to remain in the flesh is more needful for you. And being confident of this, I know that I shall remain and continue with you all for your progress and joy of faith" (NKJV).

It should provide some comfort to every Christian that even Paul may have struggled with thoughts of suicide. But Paul made the decision all of us must make, and that is why he chose life over killing himself. Deuteronomy 30:19 states, "I have set before you life and death . . . therefore choose life" (NKJV). Being a follower of Christ does not negate free will. A Christian can choose to die, but that is not God's choice. Even though he gives us freedom to choose, he tells us what to choose—life.

First Corinthians 6:19–20 states, "Do you not know that your body is the temple of the Holy Spirit who is in you, whom you have from God, and you are not your own? For you were bought at a price;

therefore glorify God in your body and in your spirit, which are God's" (NKJV). The ultimate act of bringing dishonor to what is God's is to destroy it.

If you are living amid the aftershocks of the earthquake of suicide, or if seismic tremors signal a potential quake nearby, know that you are not alone. The thoughts and feelings you are experiencing are not uncommon. For too long, suicide has been a taboo subject, one veiled in shame and guilt. There is hope. Healing and recovery are within reach.

Perhaps you as a reader are contemplating suicide. Maybe you did not consider yourself suicidal until you read this chapter. If you are a suicide survivor, you are more likely to fall victim to suicidal thoughts and feelings. Although this is not primarily an intervention book, it can provide the help you need by allowing you to realize you are not alone in your situation. The mere existence of this book shows many other people have felt what you feel. There is help available for you as a potential victim.

Make a decision right now to put the book down and call someone for help—a pastor, friend, family member, crisis line (1-800-784-2433—National Hopeline), or even 911 if you are presently at the brink of suicide.

You may have the false assumption that your family or the world would be better off without you. This is a lie. Most suicide victims believe this. Let me tell you from firsthand experience this is not true. I was not better off because of my father's death. As you read the survivor stories in this book, you will find that no one benefited from a loved one's death.

Ask yourself, *Do I want my family to go through what these families have gone through?* Your answer may be reason enough to stop you from taking this action. If you feel you are depressed, call your physician, explain that it is urgent, and say you need an appointment. Call a counselor and make an appointment. Explain that it is urgent.

Ask a family member or friend to hold you accountable. Give that person your weapon, pills, etc., until the crisis passes.

AFTERGLOW

1. Review and reconcile any myths or misconceptions you have about suicide.

2. Journal your thoughts and feelings about your loved one's suicide. List even thoughts that seem irrational.

3. Pray about what you have written.

4. Contact someone you trust to give you godly counsel and discuss what you are feeling.

CHAPTER 3

Distant Tremors: *Depression and Teen Suicide*

"I am feeble and utterly crushed;
I groan in anguish of heart" (Ps. 38:8).

A teen suicide occurs every one and one-half hours in the United States. Each year, approximately ten thousand teens and young adults, ages fifteen to twenty-four, kill themselves. While this is the reported number, the actual number of adolescent deaths by suicide is probably three to four times this number. Many times teen suicides are not reported as suicides to protect surviving family members.

Since 1960, the suicide rate for this age group has nearly tripled, making it the leading cause of death for adolescents and the second leading cause of death for college-age youth. Teen suicide is not restricted to any single socioeconomic group. Additionally, there are between one hundred thousand and two hundred thousand suicide attempts and gestures each year for this age group.

The stressors on today's teens have greatly increased, especially in the last decade. With society's push for youth to know more, be more, and do more at an earlier age, there is little time to enjoy the pleasures and carefree existence of childhood. The emotional and physical changes experienced during the teen years can lead to adolescent depression. Often teen suicide attempts stem from long-standing problems resulting from a specific event, possibly early in childhood. Impulsive, self-destructive behaviors can result from feelings of resentment, anger, or guilt.

Retaliatory abandonment and self-punishment are common motivating factors in teen suicide. When a teen feels the pain of chronic emotional abandonment by parents, suicide may be the only way the teen knows to convey his or her feeling of pain. Although self-inflicted, the aggression is aimed at the parents.

Self-punishment stems from the inability to forgive oneself for shortcomings, whether real or perceived. Many times parents expect too much of their teens, or the teens themselves set personal standards so high that they are impossible to reach. In many cases a need for affirmation is not being met within the family. Therefore, teens crave the ego boost that results from excelling at something— academics, sports, or popularity.

In a *Parade* magazine article by Diane Hales and Robert E. Hales, entitled "When a Teenager Is Sad . . . Pay Attention!" Peter Jensen, a New York child psychiatrist and director of Columbia University's Center for the Advancement of Children's Mental Health at Columbia University in New York, says, "Depression is the most common emotional problem in adolescence and the single greatest risk factor for teen suicide."[1]

This article further states the National Institute of Mental Health estimates that up to 8 percent of American teenagers suffer from major depression, girls more so than boys. Depression is a biological condition resulting from changes in brain chemistry. Depression is treatable but often difficult to recognize in teens. Many parents see changes but are reluctant to admit their child has a mental disorder. Often, depression among teenagers is passed off as moodiness or teen rebellion.

SIGNALS OF TEEN DEPRESSION

Although most teenagers exhibit some of the following warning signs, be especially alert to sudden changes in behavior.

- Apathy, intense sadness, or hopelessness
- Outbursts of anger or sudden mood swings
- Feelings of worthlessness or self-deprecation
- Expressing suicidal thoughts or death themes
- Giving away valued possessions, seemingly "in control" of life
- Changes in sleeping or eating patterns
- Withdrawal from family, friends, and activities once enjoyed
- Changes in school performance—unapproved absences, lowered grades
- Sudden disinterest in personal appearance
- Rapid weight loss or gain
- Criminal activity, substance abuse
- Inability to concentrate
- Sluggishness, passivity, allowing others to take advantage of him or her
- Excessive feelings of guilt

Any of the following situations or problems could contribute to depression and suicidal tendencies in teens.

DIVORCE

Although it seems that divorce would have the greatest affect on a young child, it is more common for divorce to profoundly affect adolescents. Because of the emotional and physical changes experienced in adolescence, a fourteen-year-old takes the divorce of his parents much harder than a four-year-old. For teens, everything is taken very personally. Teens are hypersensitive to rejection and many internalize the divorce. A girl particularly struggles with her father leaving her mother for another woman because she feels as if the father is rejecting her personally. Many times a girl will fall into a pattern of promiscuity and risk-taking behavior once her father is gone from the home.

Often teens become suspended in a state of anger because of the fallout surrounding divorce. There is usually a change in living status—a downsizing of the home, relocation out of the school district and away from friends—and the sense of stability and normalcy vanishes.

All of these factors can lead to depression. Teens live in the here and now, and they often are not able or willing to see that circumstances will change for the better in the future. Their emotional makeup during adolescence causes teens to feel everything very intensely. It is difficult for them to look beyond the immediate.

DRUG ABUSE

When drug abuse is present in the home, whether by the teen himself or by a parent or sibling, the tendency toward depression and suicide automatically increases. The presence of an alcoholic parent in the home tends to isolate the teen from peers or causes him to stay away from the house as much as possible. Teens may feel responsibility for protecting and covering for the alcoholic parent. The hopelessness surrounding alcoholism and the teen's feeling of responsibility can lead to depression. The adolescent may fall into a pattern of alcohol or drug use in an attempt to feel better, only to become even more depressed after using these substances.

SEXUAL ORIENTATION

Teens struggle, now more than ever, with questions surrounding sexual orientation. A boy who is small in stature or who is artistically or musically talented may begin to question his sexual orientation. A girl who is overweight, has a masculine body build, or is extremely athletic may have similar concerns.

The U.S. government's *Report of the Secretary's Task Force on Youth Suicide* states, "Gay youth are 2 to 3 times more likely to attempt suicide than other young people. They may comprise up to 30% of completed youth suicides annually."[2]

Even though the Bible clearly prohibits homosexuality and there is no credible scientific evidence to support homosexuality, a vulnerable or impressionable teenager who feels "gay" will probably be predisposed to suicide.

APPEARANCE AND SELF-ESTEEM

For teens, a fear of not measuring up to our culture's standards about looks, intelligence, or popularity often leads to suicide. Satan wages some remarkably effective arguments in the minds of teens and young adults to convince them they are inferior. One of the things teens desire most is to blend in with their peers and not to be singled out and labeled as "different." It takes only a few thoughtless remarks to send a young person's self-esteem to zero.

HIGH INTELLECT

The high-IQ teenager is predisposed to depression and suicidal thoughts for several reasons. Many times highly intelligent teens are extremely sensitive and unable to relate well socially. Often they are ridiculed by peers and never seem to find a place in society where they fit in. These teens have great concern and worries for global issues, philosophical questions, and burdens for the inconsistencies and injustices of society. They worry about issues that don't bother most teens.

Highly intelligent teens may expect perfectionism in themselves and others. When this is unattainable, they may feel life holds nothing for them. They may feel that because this life is so imperfect, perhaps the next life holds greater promise.

THE OVERACHIEVER AND PERFECTIONIST

Consider this scenario: a teenage girl who is always striving for perfection. If she makes anything less than an A, she is devastated. Seeing the grade of a classmate that is even one point higher than hers reduces her to tears. A grade one digit lower than what she anticipated ruins her entire day. Many times, following a test, she calls a friend to check her answers, fearing she has made a mistake. She lives in a constant state of anxiety. It will not take much for her, at some point, to become overwhelmed by this level of anxiety. She is a prime candidate for depression and suicidal tendencies.

We can look to her parents partially for the making of this overachiever. They have great expectations of her. They want her to attend an Ivy League school, preferably on a scholarship. She has older siblings who have already distinguished themselves in college and beyond—a tough act to follow. What happens if she can't keep up? There is most assuredly some other student out there who is smarter and more charming. What happens if she doesn't get the scholarship to the school of her parents' choosing? For her, and probably her parents as well, this will be unacceptable. How will she cope?

This young woman also has a highly competitive personality. Not only does she want to make the highest grades; she also has to be the prettiest and most popular. Nothing less than superlatives will do. If she and her parents could lower the bar a little by recognizing that B's are acceptable and conceding that she doesn't have to be the best at everything, it could make a big difference. Otherwise, she's headed for trouble.

THE CONTAGIOUS NATURE OF TEEN SUICIDE

Teen suicide is at epidemic proportions and is not restricted to any particular socioeconomic group. Highly affluent teens make just as many or perhaps more suicide attempts as those in lower classes. Because teens are unique in their ability to take on and live a friend's agony, they are able to visualize themselves in a similar situation. They can identify with another person's pain to the point of feeling suicide is also an option for them. Statistics show that approximately one out of every three high school students has had a friend communicate to them their thoughts of committing suicide. So it is a myth to think that teens don't come in contact with the suicidal.

In a *Time* magazine article entitled "Could Suicide Be Contagious?" John Leo reported the possibility of cluster suicide at Bryan High School near Omaha, Nebraska. Three students who knew one another casually killed themselves within a five-day period. In the three weeks following these suicides, four other youths attempted suicide but failed. Leo concluded:

> The Omaha deaths raise an obvious question: Is
> suicide contagious? Recent clusters of adolescent suicides
> suggest that the answer is yes. In a twelve-month period
> beginning in February 1983, seven teenagers in Plano,

Texas, committed suicide, four by carbon monoxide poisoning, three by guns. Five boys in New York's Westchester and Putnam counties died by their own hand in February 1984, four of them by hanging. Within the past two weeks, one student at David Prouty High School in Spencer, Mass., committed suicide; at least two schoolmates, possibly four, tried to kill themselves and failed. Researchers know very little about cluster suicides. Some may be merely coincidences; others may be self-dramatizing efforts to capture the same outpouring of sympathy that surrounded an earlier death.[3]

Although this article was written a number of years ago, teen suicide continues in ever increasing numbers. As reported by Diane Hales and Robert E. Hales, teen depression and suicidal behaviors are ongoing.

In "Unhappy in Utah," *CBS News* correspondent Sandra Hughes reported a phenomenal increase in teen suicide in that state. In 2000, sixty-one young people between the ages of five and twenty-four killed themselves in this sparsely populated state. With Utah's suicide rate ranking as the nation's ninth highest, the U.S. surgeon general and psychiatrists are looking at high performance standards set by the Mormon culture as a potential contributor to increased teen suicide.[4]

PREVENTION OF TEEN SUICIDE

Some elements of teen suicide prevention differ slightly from intervention for adults. In *The Rarest of These Is Hope: Christians Facing Difficult Times,* Harold C. Warlick states the first step in preventing adolescent suicide is to confront romantic notions of death: "Adolescents fantasize themselves beautifully laid out like Snow White while everyone comes by to exclaim how great they are. They imagine themselves the center of attention. Since they are far away from death in illness and age, they often see it as a quiet sleep. But death is not a friend . . . it is irreversible. We should take every adolescent in the church on a tour of a funeral home's operations and take every young adult to the hospital to witness an autopsy. Death is not a friend."

Second, Warlick advocates keeping the moral guidelines of the church solid and its support networks closely knit: "The influences which lead adolescents toward suicide are changing moral climates, high mobility, a high divorce rate, abuse of alcohol and other drugs, glorification of violence in the media, and the already high suicide rate. . . . As persons deal with the shock produced by abrupt changes in life, they must have some stable institution to lean on."

Warlick's third suggestion is to stop overpromising what life will be like: "Our generation is the most over-expectant generation in history. . . . Jesus never over-promised what life would be like. In his beatitudes, he started out with some blessings and ended up telling his followers what to expect. There are conditions in life we live with and there aren't any answers or magical solutions to them."[5]

&⅞ &⅞ &⅞

If you suspect a teen is depressed or suicidal, take the following steps:

1. Take depression seriously.

2. Talk to the teen. Tell him what you have noticed about his behavior that concerns you. Let the teen know you care.

3. Confront the teen regarding alcohol and drug abuse.

4. Take steps to have the teen screened for depression. Information about where to go and what to do can be obtained from your family doctor, clinic, or school counselor.

5. Be accepting of the suggestions of professionals. Be open to allowing teens to take medication for depression and talk to a counselor.

6. Lock up medications that could be deadly if taken in quantity.

7. Remove all guns from the home. Handguns were used in almost 70 percent of teen suicides in 1990. A home with a handgun is ten times more likely to have a teen suicide.

THE FAILED ATTEMPT

It is not often we have the advantage of hearing from a victim survivor. It is with thanksgiving that we hear Drew's testimony for two reasons: first, because he is alive and able to speak, and second, because he is willing to share openly and honestly about his experience and about his feelings before and after the attempt. We also hear the story from his parents' perspective.

DREW'S STORY

"Some sat in darkness and the deepest gloom" (Ps. 107:10).

"For I am about to fall, and my pain is ever with me" (Ps. 38:17).

"The actual events of December 22, 1995, are somewhat sketchy in my mind. I can remember things about that day but not necessarily the exact order in which they occurred.

"I was an eleventh grader. The fact that it was near Christmas didn't enter into my decision to kill myself. There is a theory that people try to kill themselves at Christmas because they are depressed. That isn't the way it was for me.

Sometimes people ask me if I did it because of something someone said to me or did to me. That wasn't really my experience. Looking back on that time in my life, I realize I was having some obsessive-compulsive symptoms, but I didn't really understand what was going on. I knew I felt compelled to do certain things and do them a certain way, but I wasn't sure why. It was annoying to me, but I didn't feel depressed about it.

"Basically, I was into micromanaging everything. My life purpose at that time was to make money to support a band I formed. The money I made at a part-time job went toward buying equipment. I started the band for fun because it was something I really enjoyed. Music is important to me. For me music is an emotional experience. But I felt I was really the only one in the group who was trying hard to make sure the band stayed together. Everything in my life at that time was related to that.

"I was trying to live the Christian life, but it was confusing to me. I went to church because I felt it was what I was supposed to do. There wasn't really any 'life' to my church experience. I rededicated my life that year because I felt I should. I thought it would help to do that, but I was still struggling to understand God. God and the band were important in my life, but I had them compartmentalized.

"I had a job doing cleaning for a hotel in town. I wanted to do my best with the job to please my boss. In school I was working really hard. Not necessarily to please my parents but because I thought if my grades weren't good they would say it was because of the job and make me give it up. I needed the money the job provided to support the band. I knew I couldn't handle giving up the band, so I worked really hard academically so my parents wouldn't make me stop working. I got straight A's for the first time in my life that year, but the studying took up lots of time. It was hard work to make those grades. I had always made the honor roll but not all A's.

"The control cycle I was in—of working hard and meeting self-imposed goals—got tighter and tighter. Micromanaging the work-band-school-church thing became overwhelming. I rarely allowed myself to relax. Sometimes on Sunday nights I would let myself do nothing for a few hours, but I always felt really guilty and like I should be doing something else. I just felt I had to keep myself really busy all the time. Maybe I was running from something. I don't know.

"My parents saw I was struggling, and they tried to talk to me, but I have always kept myself at a distance from them emotionally. Not because of how they are but because of how I am. I just didn't share with them what was going on inside me.

"About this time, November, I started taking a medication to help with my acne. I don't want to blame what happened on the medicine, but it is my theory that I started having suicidal thoughts after I started taking that medicine. Mentally I wasn't in a real great place anyway, and the medicine seemed to make everything worse.

"I started feeling bad if I didn't get things accomplished or didn't do it to a certain standard I had set for myself. I was on edge and nervous about a lot of things. I felt like I was ready to crack. I don't talk to people about my feelings much anyway, but with this I just didn't want to inflict my 'stuff' on anyone else. I was close to my brother, but I didn't want to burden him with what I was experiencing.

"I thought about talking to a relative I was pretty close to who lived in another town. We had talked on a deeper level before. When I rededicated my life, I wrote my relative a letter about it and opened up about myself. For whatever reason, maybe coming from a different church background, my relative didn't write back, and I felt sort of rejected or like the rededication wasn't important in this person's eyes. When I didn't get a letter back, I knew I couldn't burden this individual with what was going on in my head.

"That's when I started to dwell on things I wasn't pleased with about myself, performance-wise. I began logging my failures mentally. I would do this mental checklist. Sometimes I could check things off as completed, but I felt my performance was never good enough.

"Then my boss cut my hours at work. When this happened, it made things worse. It was just one more thing that didn't go right. It contributed to my decision to end it all. I decided to put off doing anything for one more week. I wanted to see if just one thing would go right or work out for me. That week was not a good week. I was in my own universe or felt like it. I felt totally alone. I said a few things to my dog that I couldn't say to anyone else.

"The final day there was a Christmas party at work. I was thinking more about the fact that I had to work that day. I went to my boss to talk to him about getting a different job with the hotel. He made a phone call, but the person he was trying to reach wasn't there, and it set me off. I thought, *Why can't just ONE thing work out for me?*

"At some point I went to the gym to work out. I thought it would make me feel better to be physically active. Sometime during all that I decided I would quit my job and that would free me up a little, let a little of the pressure off. Instead of calling my boss to quit, I decided to do the mature thing and go tell him in person.

"When I got there, he wasn't there. I thought, *Great, I can't even quit my job right!* I got really upset. I wanted to cry but didn't let myself. I hadn't cried in years. I really needed to cry, but society sends the message that men don't cry. It wasn't really about how my father taught me; I just felt I couldn't let myself cry.

"I remembered this bridge I had seen on the highway when I was with a friend. It was high, and I started thinking about it. I thought about taking some pills but figured it would just mess up my stomach and not kill me. There was this guy who worked with me but got fired, and I thought about calling him and trying to get a gun from him. I figured he would have one.

"I went home instead. I used to collect knives, so I got the sharpest knife I had and took my little brother's Fisher-Price tape recorder and a blank tape. I argued with my parents about something petty and I left.

"I remember wanting it to be dark before I jumped, so I drove around and waited for the darkness. I stopped by this gas station because I had a credit card for it and bought what was intended to be my last meal—Snapple and Snack Well Cookies. Some last meal!

"I sat in the car and put the tape in the recorder and talked. I said apologies to my family and others for things I regretted and left things to people. I talked until the tape ran out. By that time the darkness had come. I wasn't sure how to get to the bridge, so I had to find it. I got on the highway and drove until I saw it and then figured out how to get on it. I stopped on the bridge and sat in the car and slit my wrists with my knife. I wasn't really sure how to do it, but I wanted to bleed to death if the fall didn't kill me. My memory is blank after that.

"Past this point the details have been told to me. I guess I got out then and sat on the bridge rail. It must have been about 6:30. I left the tape in the car. The car was still running, and someone said later it ran until it was eventually out of gas. I don't really remember anything after I got on the bridge. Some truckers said they saw me sitting on the rail bleeding.

"It is strange to look back on all of it. I actually prayed about whether I was supposed to kill myself. I told God to stop me if I wasn't supposed to do it. At the time I didn't realize I was testing God by praying that way. I knew I was a Christian. The only thing that almost stopped me from jumping was thinking about my grandmothers. I guess thinking about how sad they would be is the only thing that came close to stopping me.

"It was like there were two sides of me. There was a feeling of hearing two voices, although I can't say I was really hearing voices. It was just the 'no' side grew weaker and the 'yes, do it' side was stronger. It is important to me to take personal responsibility for my actions. I don't want to blame the medicine I was taking or any person or the devil for my decision to jump. I haven't really explored whether or not I think the devil was telling me to jump. I was just in a hurry. I wanted to get it done.

"People said they saw me fall. I didn't lose consciousness or hit my head, but at the same time I don't really remember the details. A man and his wife stopped, and she diverted traffic, and he pulled me to the side of the road. He thought an eighteen-wheeler ran over my head before he got to me because he saw my head bob on the pavement.

"My memory kicks in again when I was in the hospital, but it is hazy. The first thing that came to my mind in the hospital was what a failure I was for not succeeding in killing myself. I was really, really mad that I hadn't died. I was madder than I have ever been in my life. That feeling in the hospital was worse than anything before or since my suicide attempt. I remember being so mad and thinking, *Once I get out of here, I'll do it right!* I was mad at God for not letting me die. My emotions were so strong, very intense.

"My injuries were extensive. When I jumped, I landed on my feet and basically broke every bone in my feet. The impact broke both heels and ankles, my left wrist and elbow, a bone in my right hand, and my pelvis. A number of vertebrae were cracked and the L-3 vertebra was destroyed, splintering into my spinal cord.

"For a few days I was paralyzed from the waist down. Then my left leg started having some motor impulses, at which point my spinal injury was termed incomplete. I was transferred to a hospital in another state and was there for two or two-and-a-half months while they tried to rebuild me. At some point while I was in that hospital, I stopped thinking about trying to kill myself again.

"It took several more years of rehabilitation. Part of it was at another hospital, and then once I got home, I did rehabilitation work at the gym. I continued to have surgeries to try to rebuild my feet and back. I basically have no feeling in my right leg from the knee down. I should probably be doing some rehabilitation work now, but the pain is just too much in my feet. I'm in pain constantly when I'm standing.

"I finished high school and took a year off to do rehab. I did my freshman year of college at home because physically I was not at a place where I could be on my own. Then I transferred to another college in-state. I'm a junior now. I'm still deciding what I want to do with my life. I'm still trying to understand the 'God stuff' and how that fits into my life. I think my faith will be part of what I do ultimately. Maybe not professionally but in some way I want it to be part of what I do—that and music. Even if it is just for me personally, I want to work around or with music in some way, maybe a recording studio.

"I found a church I really like. It is a postmodern church with an interactive preaching style. I really like that. It's cool. The church is small but growing. I was leading a small group in my church at home, and now I'll do my small group in my new church. The pastor there is discipling me, taking me through this discipleship course. I was in a discipleship group before the suicide attempt, but now I understand better what discipleship is about.

"My brother tried to make me feel guilty because it hurt him that we were close and I didn't tell him what I was going to do. He's had a hard time with that. My parents never made me feel guilty. They were very careful not to make me feel guilty.

"I've dealt with feeling that I died when I jumped but was still trapped here, like I was a living dead person. The jump didn't kill me, and so I was still stuck here suffering. I've experienced a kind of mourning or grieving, but it is for the loss of my physical ability, for the disability I have now because of my injuries. I deal with that daily, but it is getting better.

"If friends and my family hadn't cared so much, I probably would have tried to kill myself again, unless God himself had stepped in. I can't count the number of people who played a part in my recovery. People I didn't know and who didn't know me were praying for me. There was a part of me that felt so undeserving of all the help I got.

"Lots of people have told me that my life was spared because God had something important for me to do. At first, that idea scared me because it felt like pressure, like everyone was watching me to see this great thing happen. At first I thought, *What do I have to do to live up to this?* Now I am more comfortable with the idea. I think I will do something, but not anything really big. I'm getting better at seeing and understanding God's will for my life. Maybe now I'm not quite as worried about missing his will for me.

"There is one thing I want to make sure people understand, and this is that suicide is a very personal thing. No one could have done *anything* to stop me. My decision didn't have to do with anything outside me. A lot of people say suicide is a selfish thing, but I don't believe that. They need to understand that the person contemplating suicide has done *everything* to make himself feel better and nothing has worked and this is the last bit—the last thing left to do. I've never bought the idea that suicide is a selfish thing. To me, if the person were selfish, he *wouldn't* try to kill himself because he would be thinking self-preservation.

"Suicide is always personal, and there's not some formula for the decision. It's a personal decision and it comes from within. I can't emphasize that enough—*it's personal*.

"I would like to get it across to the families and friends of suicide victims that it's not about something they did or didn't do. They need to stop blaming themselves for their loved one's decision to die. It's not about them. It's about the individual.

"I knew my family loved me and I loved them, but the suicide feelings overtook my love for my family and their love for me. The suicide feelings were just stronger than the love.

"I don't mind talking about my suicide attempt if people ask me. If they ask, I will tell them, but I don't just go around broadcasting the fact that I tried to kill myself. The only time it bothers me to think about my suicide attempt is when I relive it or remember parts of what happened when I am by myself. Then I get scared. I'm still working through all that happened. It's a process."

DREW'S STORY FROM HIS PARENTS' PERSPECTIVE

When did your son attempt suicide?

PETE: All of our lives changed forever on December 22, 1995.

Did you suspect something was going on with Drew before his suicide attempt?

JEAN: I knew there were personality changes. We knew he was dealing with depression. He was on antidepressants for a while, but the doctor took him off the medicine six months before the attempt because he was still growing and there was concern about the medicine's effect on his growth. Once he was diagnosed with depression, the thought of suicide was always in the back of my mind. I told his brother and his closest friends to let me know if he ever mentioned anything that sounded suicidal. They assured me he was fine. They didn't see any clues, but he was hiding his thoughts from everyone.

PETE: I didn't see it at all. Suicide didn't cross my mind. I knew Drew was superactive—involved in church, school, and working. But I just thought he was maturing and growing into a man. He'd just rededicated his life to the Lord. He seemed like he had it all together. Later, in talking to psychiatrists, we learned that adolescents often hide and mask depression and suicidal thoughts much more than adults. His depression didn't manifest itself as it would in an adult. It was helpful to us that the psychiatrist explained Drew's constant activity as an attempt to outrun his depression.

JEAN: Drew was dealing with some obsessive-compulsive disorder symptoms. Everything had to be done before he would go to bed. I remember going into his room to encourage him to go to bed, and he would be on his knees beside his bed praying through the prayer list from his youth group. It had to be done before he would allow himself to go to bed.

At work he would do anything the boss asked and do it to the extreme. I shared this with a friend, and she said he sounded like the perfect teenager, but I knew it was too much. Perhaps because I had dealt with depression myself or because of the mama/son connection, I had concern for what Drew might do.

Pete, you are a counselor. Counseling teens and college students is your job. After Drew's suicide attempt, did you ever think why didn't I see this coming?

PETE: The majority of the college students I counsel have the more classic signs of depression. They sleep through classes or cut classes and withdraw from all activities. Drew was just the opposite. He turned on all the jets and went so fast that I completely missed it. He seemed mature and wasn't into alcohol, sex, egging people's houses, or harassing other kids. He was almost like a little adult. I know that firstborn children are driven and goal oriented, and it just seemed like, wow, this is great! He's maturing!

JEAN: But he didn't associate with very many peers. He tried to do things with the church youth group but never seemed to find his niche.

PETE: Drew became an introvert's introvert.

JEAN: This began around puberty. Prior to that he was very outgoing and always doing things with friends.

PETE: He played basketball on the church league and did what he was supposed to, but he seemed to resent his participation. He wasn't a jock, and because he was trying for perfection and couldn't get there, he had an attitude.

What fears did you have following his suicide attempt?

JEAN: Initially, we were just consumed with keeping him alive because of his extensive physical injuries from the attempt. He had many, many brushes with death because he was so injured.

PETE: Drew was so physically broken that if he was going to die it was going to be because of his physical injuries rather than through another suicide attempt.

JEAN: Later, of course, we had concerns. Even as recently as a few years ago when he still wasn't on the right balance of medication, he would sometimes make statements that sounded very suicidal in nature. But he had made a promise to his counselor that he would not attempt again without calling him first, and he took that promise seriously. We were constantly concerned but realized that if he was bound and determined to attempt again, that pledge wasn't going to stop him. We came to the point where we had to release him.

PETE: Any suicide attempt is serious. When a person takes an overdose of Tylenol and has to have his stomach pumped, yes, there needs to be concern, but physically that person is normal, once the crisis is over. In Drew's case we were dealing with a crushed spine, crushed ankles, and paralysis. Physically, it was as if he had been through a war—plus, he had done it to himself. I think because Jean and I were forced into dealing with life-and-death situations about his spine, his brain, walking or not walking, thoughts of his being a quadriplegic or paraplegic—initially that took precedence over fears that he would attempt again. If Drew's suicide attempt had been an overdose of Tylenol, we would have had him in sessions with a counselor and a psychiatrist. It would have been dodging the bullet, but essentially we would have gone on with life. But because of Drew's injuries, to this day our lives have never been the same.

JEAN: It is only by the grace of God that we don't constantly live on pins and needles.

PETE: I remember when Drew got to the point in his rehabilitation that he was going to learn to drive with hand controls. I thought, *We can't let him do that.* But his psychiatrist said this was a good goal for him, and if he was going to attempt again there was nothing we could do to stop him. If he was adamant about self-destruction, he was going to do it tomorrow, next month, next year, and we couldn't chain him to a desk and never let him do anything again. We had to release him and realize that we had done everything possible and couldn't put him under lock and key 24/7. If we had chosen to allow ourselves to live under that kind of anxiety, it would have destroyed our marriage and our family. We either had to release Drew or destroy our family and ourselves.

JEAN: We know there was supernatural intervention in the fact that Drew survived at all. He tried a three-way approach to suicide: slit wrists, the jump from a bridge, and landing in the middle of interstate traffic. If one thing didn't kill him, something else would, and it should have, but God intervened. It has been phenomenal to see what God has done.

PETE: I think Drew decided that he *wanted* to live, and because of that, he did everything the counselor and psychiatrist asked him to do.

JEAN: They got Drew to read, journal, and keep a daily planner. He was able to become a lot more reasonable about his personal goals. If he didn't reach all his goals that day, he could let it go until another day.

PETE: Also, the psychiatrist put him back on an antidepressant, and that made a difference because he definitely had a chemical imbalance.

JEAN: Drew got very agitated in the fall about some of his classes. We tried to convince him to go back on an antidepressant, but he said he didn't like the way it made him feel.

PETE: He had gotten so used to that anxious feeling of go-go-go that he didn't like the fact that the antidepressant leveled him out. I feel it is such a shame that American society still has such a poor attitude about antidepressants. You can take any other kind of medicine for any other condition, and people will say, *I'm glad that medicine is helping your arthritis or headache or blood pressure,* but if a college student walks into the dorm room and sees his new roommate has a Prozac or Zoloft bottle on his desk, he immediately thinks, *This guy is crazy, and he's going to kill me in my sleep.* Then, if you tell your parents, they say, *We can't have you rooming with a guy who's on Prozac.* But if the same roommate has only one leg and is on crutches or has an insulin pump, those same parents say, *Be kind to him and see if you can do anything to help him.*

JEAN: We as a society just haven't come very far with understanding and accepting emotional illness.

Let's branch out a little from that thought. Does the Christian community have an even more closed-minded attitude toward emotional and mental illness?

PETE: Yes, definitely. You hear pastors say, *You don't need psychiatrists or antidepressants.* I don't think that is what they really mean.

I think these pastors want people to look to Jesus for ultimate healing and salvation, but it comes across as, *Don't get professional help*. There are so many self-help books out there that I think these pastors want to get the message across that there is no salvation through psychiatry. I also feel people need to select a counselor who is biblically based—someone who actually quotes Scripture during counseling sessions. Depression is not attitudinal, and it can require professional intervention.

JEAN: Another thing we discovered during Drew's recovery is there really are not many programs available, at least in this community, for teenagers with emotional or mental needs. There was a day program at the mental health association, but it was mostly for elderly people; and the facility was not set up to deal with Drew's physical problems. We were hoping for a program where Drew could be cared for during the day and get schooling, but all the programs of this type had been cancelled because of lack of funding, and there was nothing available. This was probably our lowest point post-attempt because there was nowhere to turn for the kind of help we needed.

PETE: On top of this, our insurance totally denied coverage. They paid not one penny. They said any self-induced injury was not covered. Eventually, we had to file for bankruptcy.

JEAN: But we knew God was with us, and it was unbelievable how people came to our aid. The money was always there when Drew needed more surgery.

PETE: For the first time I understood what it means to be part of the body of Christ and to benefit from the ministry of the body. People who didn't even know Drew from our state and neighboring states gave money and sent cards. Drew saw how much people cared. Before his suicide attempt he had withdrawn so much he didn't even accept love from us, his parents. He just saw our love as harassment. But it was impossible for him not to see how much people cared when they were paying for his surgeries and remodeling our house to accommodate his disabilities.

JEAN: Several pastors have really ministered to Drew. One, especially, helped him understand that returning to suicidal thoughts as a way to solve his problems is like flirting with an old girlfriend. It had to be his choice to approach life differently and to handle problems without returning to a familiar but destructive way.

What advice would you give parents who suspect their child is suicidal or parents living with a failed-attempt child?

JEAN: For those living with a failed attempt or those who suspect their child is depressed:

1. Pray.

2. Get counseling for your child.

3. Work with doctors and psychiatrists to get the right combination of medication. Don't be afraid to put your child on medication. Don't let pride or fear of what people will say keep you from doing what you need for your child. You have to bring the child back up to a level of being able to reason with him before therapy will do any good.

4. Watch for the layers in your children. What could tip them over the edge to the point of being suicidal? We feel Drew's complexion problems affected his self-esteem and that factored into the equation. Also, the obsessive-compulsive tendencies and perfectionism played a role. If your child is reclusive, dressing differently from his peers, working too hard, or non communicative, beware. Any of these behaviors could be signs of depression.

Are there any Bible verses that became special to you during Drew's recovery?

JEAN: The Lord was faithful to give us many verses, especially during the first two or three months. I had an incredible sense of God's nearness.

PETE: The Lord spoke to me through the Book of Daniel where it says God shut the mouths of the lions. It doesn't say God killed the lions or kept Daniel from being thrown in the den, but he sealed their mouths so Daniel was not destroyed.

At what point were you able to arrive at joy?

JEAN: Believe it or not, we actually laughed a lot during the months that Drew was in the hospital. He had a wonderful male nurse who is a Christian. He ministered to us, and we still keep in touch with him.

PETE: We experienced constant small victories along the way that brought us joy, but the day we moved Drew to college and he was independent for the first time since the attempt, for me that was joyous. Jean and I looked at each other in the parking lot and said, *Look how far God has brought him and us.* Drew still has multiple handicaps, but if God can raise him from the dead, we trust him to take care of the little details. God has been faithful to protect our marriage, too, because in so many cases like ours, one parent eventually blames the other. That didn't happen, and we know it was totally because of God's grace.*

ॐ ॐ ॐ

"He brought them out of darkness and the deepest gloom and broke away their chains. Let them give thanks to the LORD for his unfailing love and his wonderful deeds for men" (Ps. 107:14–15).

AFTERGLOW

1. Check for your "blind spots" regarding your loved one's or teenager's potential for suicide. Is there more going on than what you are seeing?

2. If your teenager is struggling with sexual orientation questions, discuss these questions: Can you think of another "species" that does not have the ability to reproduce? If homosexuality is genetic rather than a learned behavior, why is a homosexual union unable to reproduce?

3. If you have a teenage son who is struggling with sexual orientation, read James Dobson's *Bringing Up Boys.*

4. Be intentional about elevating your teen's self-esteem. Focus on positive qualities about your teen rather than the negatives.

---

* Drew graduated Phi Beta Kappa from college in the spring of 2002. His future plans include a move to Atlanta, Georgia, to pursue a career in music or media.

5. Know who your teenager's friends are. Make your home a place where your teen feels comfortable spending time with friends.

6. Be available to talk over problems with your teen. Keep the lines of communication open.

CHAPTER 4

❧

Surveying the Devastation: *The Survivors*

"I have great sorrow and continual grief in my heart"
(Rom. 9:2 NKJV).

*L*ike an earthquake registering off the Richter scale, suicide brings immediate devastation to the lives of those in its path. Obviously, for the actual suicide victim, loss of life is the ultimate consequence. The effects of an earthquake are strongest in a broad zone surrounding the epicenter. The family, left behind, is at the epicenter of the quake. For these loved ones, the destruction is multifaceted. Although everyone who knows the victim, whether casually or intimately, is affected, the immediate family suffers the greatest damage.

People who have experienced an earthquake firsthand say it seems as if the quake lasts forever, even if it is only seconds. When the shifting earth is finally still, everywhere you look there is damage. The realization of what has happened barely settles in before the aftershocks begin. You find yourself thinking, *What's next?*

Suicide is no different. The effects of one person's action seem to go on for a lifetime and beyond. Some people view suicide as an act of ultimate selfishness. Others see it almost as an act of self-sacrifice.

Either way, in a moment when reason shifts askew and a troubled individual decides to "end it all," generations to come tremble under the rippling effects of self-murder.

As surface ground cracks appear along earthquake fault lines, so the survivors' world shatters into a million pieces. Those who remain encounter the aftershocks of isolation, anger, guilt, rejection, betrayal, grief, and loss. Loved ones are left to sift through the debris of the suicidal quake.

Life changes in an instant for suicide survivors. One moment, they are blissfully traveling down the road of life, and the next, an event happens that opens the earth in a yawning chasm before them. As with the survivors of an actual earthquake, suicide families are in shock, simply existing in the wake of the destruction.

For earthquake survivors, locating food, water, and shelter is the first order of business following the quake. Standing in front of the rubble that was once their home does nothing to restore the edifice, and looking beyond the present seems impossible. So it is for suicide survivors. The challenge of the first few days and weeks is to survive while reality settles in.

Someone described suicide survival as similar to losing a filling from a tooth: you know the filling is missing, but you continue to put your tongue in the hole until it is raw and bleeding. Although it causes pain, you can't stop yourself from revisiting the gaping hole over and over again.

As if the death of a loved one were not enough to handle, suicide survivors must deal with the social stigma attached to suicide. In general, people do not know how to react to or comfort suicide families. Suicide is akin to a sort of social leprosy.

Families are seen as unclean because of the act of the victim. A shadow is cast across the entire family as if something must be wrong with them all. Surely other family members will fall prey to this horrible means of death as well as by sheer association. And then there is the thought that perhaps the whole suicide idea might be "catching." If you associate with the family, are you putting yourself and your family at risk of developing a suicidal mind-set? A far-fetched and unrealistic idea? Yes. An uncommon thought pattern for those on the outside looking in? No.

Survivors can expect people to say unkind or thoughtless things following a suicide death. This can be true with any death. When people don't know what to say but feel they are expected to say something, their comments can be hurtful. It is not uncommon to hear any of the following: "He'll be better off," "We all knew she was a little crazy," or, "He'll burn in hell for this."

As with any death, people often feel talking about it will upset the family so they avoid the subject. What they don't understand is the survivors need to talk about what has happened. Healing will never take place if the gaping wound of suicide pain is covered without being allowed to heal from the inside out.

Suppose an earthquake seriously damages the foundation of a home, yet the house appears otherwise intact. There are obvious cracks, but instead of making the necessary inspection and repairs, the owner opts for stuccoing over the damaged foundation. From the exterior the repairs seem complete. But one day an aftershock strikes the already insecure foundation, and the entire house comes crashing down.

Waiting to address the damage done by suicide only postpones the inevitable. Talking about what has happened is a vital part of the healing process. Unless you have experienced it personally, it is difficult to understand the intensity of the pain.

A childbirth analogy comes to mind. Men can never really understand the pain of childbirth because they haven't experienced it. A husband can stand by his wife's bedside during labor and delivery, hold her hand, be supportive, and wince in sympathy, but he can never really feel the pain. So those who have not lived a suicide experience cannot imagine the depth of the survivors' pain.

Huge chunks of unreconciled pain are scattered in the path of recovery for suicide families or failed-attempt families. While picking through the rubble, the ordinary things of life must go on. Amid the chaos of second-guessing and "what if's," survivors must deal with the mundane issues of the funeral, finances, paperwork, probate, and insurance claims; or in the case of failed attempts, recovery, rehabilitation, counseling, and medication.

Quite often insurance companies are unwilling to pay on the life insurance policies of suicide victims. If they do pay, it may be only a portion of the amount, or the family is in for a long battle to get anything at all. The world doesn't slow down for anyone's grief, but for suicide survivors life takes on a surreal quality. While trying to make sense out of the senseless, they are bombarded with a tidal wave of emotions and practical matters demanding their attention.

Survivors are plagued with unanswered questions. One of the greatest struggles for the surviving family and friends is wondering if the victim had some secret or some private activities that they didn't know about. They reason, *There had to be something else because what we do know is not sufficient cause for the suicide.*

Many people feel they can handle the grief better if they can discover the victim was terminally ill or hiding some other secret or failure. Feelings of rejection and abandonment swirl around the questions: *Didn't he know how much this would hurt us? Didn't he care?*

Guilt plays heavily in the equation. *Why didn't I see this coming? What if I had been more observant? If I had said or done something differently, could I have prevented this?*

Many times I counsel individuals who are hung up on the "what if's" to the point of being illogical. They constantly replay the events with thoughts of, *If only I hadn't gone to work that day* or *if only I had come straight home instead of stopping by the store.*

Although it is illogical to believe they could have controlled the circumstances or prevent the suicide with an altered activity pattern, it is also very normal for survivors to be stuck at this point for a while. It is important for the survivors to come to the point of understanding the victim would not blame them for their activities on the day of the suicide. The victim was probably so intent on the act that he or she planned it around their activities in order to be successful.

Eventually anger becomes an issue for survivors. It is almost impossible to get around feeling angry with medical professionals, your loved one, yourself, God, or the world in general. Anger at God stems from the questions, Why did God allow this? Did he cause it? or Is it what he wanted? If you are angry at God, go ahead and tell him. He is more than able to handle all your anger and continue to love you in the process.

Ultimately, you must realize that God did not choose for the person to die. The decision to die was the victim's choice. God allows us to make choices about our lives, and his will does not override our free will.

It is appropriate and normal to feel anger and to express it. Families often place blame on medical professionals: a doctor treating a person with medication for depression—Why didn't the medicine help? a counselor or psychologist—Why didn't you talk her out of doing it? paramedics—Why didn't they save his life?

Angry thoughts toward your loved one bring on complex emotions. It is not unusual to experience feelings of rejection, abandonment, betrayal, and fear in addition to anger. Amid this combination of emotions comes guilt from feeling angry with a loved one who is no longer alive.

It is not uncommon for family members to experience anger, confusion, and frustration to the point of feeling suicidal themselves. For some, it is a feeling of wanting to be with the loved one so much that immediate death seems to be the way to accomplish this. Others have the attitude, *If it was good enough for Daddy, it's good enough for me.* Having these thoughts does not mean remaining family members will act on them. It is important to understand you can make the choice to handle your pain in a different manner.

You can suppose and reckon and reason endlessly, but you will never come up with a really good answer to why the loved one chose death over life. Even if survivors are able to gather all the pieces to the puzzle and fit them together, they never can see the full picture as seen through the eyes of the victim. It doesn't do much good to continually speculate because, no matter what the reasons, you can't bring the loved one back.

EXPLAINING SUICIDE TO CHILDREN

From personal experience I can say that children should not be shielded from the truth of suicide. Often adults feel they are doing children a favor or protecting them by leaving them ignorant immediately following a suicide. This is never wise. Evading the truth, speaking in veiled terms, or telling outright lies about someone who has committed suicide will do more damage than good, particularly if a child hears or overhears the truth from someone else. For a child, not knowing the truth can be more terrifying and painful than being told. Just because the subject of suicide is difficult to approach doesn't mean it should be sidestepped. Being evasive about suicide with a child can cause children to wonder later if they can trust you about other issues.

The amount of information you give children can vary with their age and level of understanding. Some children will be content with little explanation. Others will ask a multitude of questions, and they should be allowed to do so without being silenced or put off. Either way, be sure the answers you give are straightforward and honest.

In my case, the delay of several days in telling me my father's death was suicide resulted in great anger. I encourage adults to be honest with children about suicide and realize they may feel all the conflicting emotions adults do, in addition to others.

A child may feel any of the following:

- Abandonment. The person killed himself because he didn't love me.

- Responsibility. My mother's death is my fault. If I had behaved better or loved her more, she wouldn't have killed herself.

- Fear. I might die, too. Someone else I love is going to die. Who will take care of me?

- Guilt. Because I was angry with the person or wished him dead at some point. A child often verbalizes or thinks *I wish you were dead,* regarding an adult in a moment of anger.

- Confusion. What is going to happen next? Will I have to change schools? Will we have to move? What does this all mean?
- Embarrassment. What will other people think about my dead loved one or about my family and me? Why are people staring at me?
- Anger. Toward the person who died, God, or other adults.
- Loneliness. No one wants to talk about what happened.
- Denial. Pretending nothing has happened.
- Numbness. Can't feel any emotion.
- Desire to escape. I want to go somewhere else. I wish this would all go away. Escaping into a fantasy world.
- Sadness.

TELLING CHILDREN: THE APPROACH

Remain calm. In the case of suicide, this is difficult to do, but if you feel you are going to come unglued, try to deal as much as possible with your own feelings first. Children are going to watch you for clues on how to respond and deal with the news. If you are distraught and falling apart emotionally, they will follow your example. If you just can't bring yourself to be the bearer of the news, the child still needs to be told. The second choice after the parent is someone the child has a close relationship with or someone who can relay the news honestly. A grandparent, minister, or Sunday school teacher would be a good choice.

In the case of a parent suicide, it is absolutely imperative that the surviving parent is present when the child is told. This keeps the child from wondering if the other parent is also dead or from wondering if the other parent knows about the suicide. After the child is told, the parent needs to follow up short-term with, "Do you have any questions?" "What do you think this means for us as a family?" "What do you think people will think about your dad?" "How are you doing?" or, "What are you feeling?" The parent also needs to reassure the child that he or she is loved and is in no way responsible for the loved one's suicide decision.

Talk to your children as soon as possible. Speak in a normal voice and state the facts. Ask your children what they already know, and dispel rumors and misinformation. It is much better for the child to hear the news from you than to overhear it from someone else.

Give age-appropriate information. Remember, a child's attention span is about the same in minutes as his age. For a five-year-old, about five minutes worth of talking about the incident is all he can absorb. Use simple language, but make sure what you are saying is the truth. Avoid statements like "Grandpa has gone to sleep," "God needed your brother in heaven," or, "Daddy has gone on a long trip."

Any of these explanations will cause a child to have fears. The "gone to sleep" approach will cause the child to be fearful of going to sleep or of having anyone else sleep. Saying God needed the person in heaven will cause the child to blame God for her brother's death or no longer view God as a loving heavenly Father. Don't present God as being responsible for the death. "Gone on a long trip" will cause the child to expect Daddy to return some day, thus delaying the acceptance of reality.

In addition to vague information, avoid giving too much explanation. If the information is verbose and convoluted, the child will cease to listen before absorbing what is being said.

Cushion the bad news with good. Start by talking about how the person lived (if something positive). Mention good qualities about the person. Say, "Many people loved him and thought a lot of him." If you are telling a child about a parent, say, "One of the most wonderful things your mother did was give you life." Then talk about life being precious and fragile—a gift. Follow this with the facts of the suicide. It is important to give accurate information.

Realize fears. Children could immediately feel fearful on hearing the news, but they will probably feel anger or shock initially. Physical touch—a hug, an arm around the shoulders, or a hand on the back—will be helpful in comforting the child.

Allow children to ask questions. Let children ask any questions they want to about the death. No question should be considered silly or "unaskable." Listen carefully and patiently, then respond. If you can't answer the child's question honestly, say, "I don't know the answer to that question."

Tell children it is all right to feel sad. Let children know grieving is normal in the case of a suicide death or any death. Crying is part of grief. However, providing a familiar routine as soon as possible following the loss will allay fears and give children a sense of stability.

You may have to retell later. If children experience a period of denial, they may ask to be told again, or you may see the need to tell them again. Pretending the suicide didn't happen will stop the grief process and be detrimental.

It is very important to talk to children and help them understand that all the conflicting emotions they are feeling are normal, considering the circumstances. Children need to be able to express what they are feeling or keep to themselves for a period of time, if they wish. Children need to know that the person who died loved them, but he didn't realize how much his death would hurt his loved ones. Children especially need to know nothing they said or didn't say (or did or didn't do) caused the death. They also need to be assured the complicated emotions they are feeling will lessen, and in time, they will feel better.

Dawn's Story

The fact that Dawn arrived for the interview on her motorcycle spoke volumes about the ability of this mother to recover from the death of her beloved son. She stood at my door proclaiming the beauty of the spring day, sporting a bright smile and a lively personality. It was not until well into the interview that her eyes took on the haunting look of a suicide survivor and I saw the depth of her pain.

Dawn's twenty-three-year-old son, Levy, committed suicide on April 16, 1997. Although she is able to embrace life in the midst of her pain, Dawn states, "There is not a day, almost not an hour, that I don't think about Levy. He enjoyed life and was fun to be around. That is why it is still so strange to me that he took his own life. How could someone so full of life choose death?"

Here is Dawn's account of her experience as a suicide survivor.

"Growing up, Levy lived what I term a 'charmed' life. He was popular, good-looking, a football star, student council member, Beta Club member, and he had a great personality. He went to college on a full academic scholarship. I think things had gone so well for him that when he started to encounter failure in any form in his life, he couldn't handle it.

"His first taste of failure was being charged with DUI the summer following high school graduation and losing his driver's license. Then, his sophomore year in college, he was suspended for a semester and lost his scholarship. He had plans to return to college, but never did.

"Just before his suicide; his marriage was in trouble. I believe he saw this as another failure. He and his wife separated. During the course of the separation, he insinuated to her he was going to commit suicide by saying things like, 'You better take a long, hard look at me,' as if implying he wouldn't be around much longer. She told us she thought he was suicidal, but neither she nor we believed it was anything to be concerned about.

"My husband and I recognized Levy was dealing with some depression. One day he would seem depressed, and the next he would be fine. After his death, we discovered he had several books on depression. I believe he didn't seek help for his depression because he was smart and thought he could 'cure' himself. For him, it would have been a black mark to have to seek help.

"A few days before his suicide, our daughter-in-law called us and said Levy was at their house and 'talking out of his head.' My husband and I went to see him and realized he was very depressed. I knew his marital problems were part of the problem. I told him not everyone gets it right the first time. My husband and I had both been married previously, and I told him it wasn't the end of the world. Levy said, 'I can understand in my mind, but I can't understand it with my heart.' We talked to him about his suicide threat, and he looked me in the face and said, 'Mother, I would never do anything like that!'

"I told Levy I would feel better if he came home with us so

I wouldn't worry about him and could get some sleep. My husband and I were going out of town the next day and I wanted Levy with us that night. He came to our house. I gave him some homemade soup and cornbread. He was gone the next morning when we got up because he had to be at work early. That night was the last time we saw him alive.

"The next night, he went out partying with some friends. He stayed out all night at a bar, but refused to smoke marijuana with the others. He was dealing with some substance abuse problems and was attending NA meetings. I don't believe he was planning to take his life, because what was the point in not smoking marijuana if he planned to kill himself? About 5:00 a.m., he called his wife and told her he was getting a ride to the house and wanted her to drive him to work. She didn't want to be there when he arrived, so she woke their two little girls, ages three and five months, and was putting them in the car to leave when he got there. I don't blame her for leaving. Levy had been drinking, and his personality totally changed when he was drinking.

"I think the fact she was leaving was more than he could take. It was a breaking point. He needed a ride to work and thought he might lose his job if he didn't get to work or was late. I don't believe he was thinking clearly.

"After she left, he went into their house and called a friend, but couldn't get in touch with him. He left a message on the answering machine saying, 'I need to talk to you' and then went into their bedroom and shot himself in the head with my husband's gun. He never asked us for the gun, so we believe he just took it and had had it for a while. From his position in the room, it appeared he watched himself in the mirror as he killed himself. He had taken an EMT course and apparently from that training knew exactly where to shoot himself to ensure death. His was not a cry for help. He really intended to be successful.

"It was probably six hours before my daughter-in-law found him. She was concerned and called the house a number of times, but never got an answer. After she called his place of business and found he had never come to work that day, she decided to go to the house. She had a feeling all was not right, so she left the girls in the car. As she approached the bedroom, she saw his hand and knew from the color that he was dead. She ran from the room and called 911.

"My mother made the call to me. She said simply, 'You need to come home. Something horrible has happened.' She didn't want to tell me over the phone. I just had a feeling and I asked her if it was Levy and if he was dead. When she said 'yes,' I ran screaming through the hotel hall. There is no other pain like the pain I felt when I heard Levy was dead. You can't imagine the depth of the pain until you have experienced it personally. Several ladies in the hospitality room helped me. One tried to calm me down while the other went to find my husband on the golf course. When they found him, they only told him I needed him. He never dreamed the news was about Levy. Although not his biological child, Levy was his son. It was as difficult for him as it was for me to hear the news.

"We were flown home on a private jet. I will always be grateful for that. I'm not sure I could have dealt with the airport and a commercial flight. All I knew was I wanted to get home and see Levy. We went to the hospital, but they would not let me see him until they released the body to the mortuary. That was very hard for me.

"In a way, it was probably good we were not in town when it happened. I'm sure I would immediately have gone to the house, and I didn't need to see what was there. I was spared seeing that.

"The question that has haunted me the most about Levy's suicide is 'Why did he give up on life?' Levy wasn't a quitter, and to me, his suicide seemed to be quitting. Several months after his death, I had a dream. I have always dreamed a lot and vividly. After the suicide, I didn't dream for a while. When I did, I dreamed Levy was sitting beside me dressed in clothes I recognized. I believe the purpose of this dream was to help me with my grief. In the dream Levy said, 'You are looking at this from your point of view. You see my suicide as quitting; I saw it as not knowing how to give up.' That dream helped me to understand the suicide from his perspective.

"My feeling that Levy's death had changed me, bothered me. For months, my thoughts were jumbled, and I couldn't concentrate. During that time, I thought in poetry. Some of it I wrote down. Some of the poetry came and went in my mind without my ever recording it. Levy wrote lots of poetry. Perhaps my thinking in poetry was a connection to him.

"As part of my recovery, I read lots of books. *Handbook to Grief* was very helpful to me. Through reading this book, I learned a great deal about grief. My husband told me I sighed often. In reading, I discovered sighing is a symptom of grieving. *My Son, My Son* by Iris Bolton was also very good. In one part, a preacher comes to her and tells her to look for gifts in the midst of her grief. I am thankful I have been able to do that. Having my grandchildren is one thing that helps.

"The Survivors of Suicide support group has also been very helpful. I don't know how people who can't talk about what they are going through can make it. In the beginning, I went to the group because I needed help. Now, four years later, I go to help other people.

"Losing a child is the worst thing you can experience, but you have to make the choice of how to allow something to affect you. You talk and work through it until you can come to terms with it. Talking and being with other survivors is so important. Sometimes you think you are crazy. You have some of the strangest thoughts, but talking to others who are going through the same experience helps you realize you aren't crazy.

"It is still very hard. When I look at my grandchildren, I think how unfair it is for them to grow up without a daddy. They know their daddy shot himself, but I don't think they understand the concept of suicide. I have a dream to one day write a book to help children understand suicide. If I can do that, maybe I will be making something good out of my son's death, turning tragedy into triumph, and giving a gift to my grandchildren. I just believe if Levy had realized how many people's lives would be affected by his suicide, he wouldn't have done it."

BEING THERE FOR THE SURVIVORS

Many Christians do not know how to respond to suicide. In their ignorance they often do more harm than good. Christians often feel compelled to pass judgment on the circumstances of the death and speculate about whether the victim is in heaven or hell. This is never appropriate. God is the only righteous judge, and the status of the soul of the deceased is in his hands. Church leaders especially need to leave judgment to God. Many survivors have turned their backs on church and God following a judgmental statement by an overly pious pastor.

One individual turned to a cult following the sermon preached at the funeral of a relative, a suicide victim. "I want nothing to do with a religion that condemns my relative to hell for choosing suicide. How could that pastor possibly know my relative's heart and relationship with God?"

Friends can be the most helpful to the survivors by being available and listening. Don't feel you have to inform or justify. Because suicide is an awkward, uncomfortable subject, people are tempted to avoid the truth. Hiding from the truth only makes grief recovery more difficult. Simply be there to listen and comfort with your presence.

In listening, you should be prepared to hear and accept a wide range of emotions. You may be uncomfortable with the intensity of these emotions. But it is important for survivors to express themselves without being silenced. Don't try to calm survivors down or cut short their expression of emotion. The freedom to work through anger and grief in a personal way will hasten the healing process.

Realize the most difficult period for the family is probably still weeks away. During the initial period of shock, the survivors are not feeling many of the emotions they will feel later. You may meet the greatest need six to eight weeks after the death. One of the most crucial parts of suicide recovery is the opportunity for survivors to talk about what happened and to express their feelings.

AFTERGLOW

1. Begin to release responsibility for your loved one's death.

2. As a survivor, examine the targets of your anger. Make a list of whom you are angry with and why. Pray, asking God to begin to diffuse your anger.

3. Monitor children survivors closely. Initiate conversation regarding their feelings and fears.

4. Provide a fun outlet for children even if you have to enlist the help of others—a trip to a theme park, mountain hike, or an afternoon of swimming with friends.

5. For those looking for ways to minister to suicide survivors, think of practical ways to help—meal preparation, transporting children, home repairs, errands, etc.

6. Make a list of plans for your future, including short-term and long-term goals. Include necessary plans to implement and complete those goals.

Bent but Not Destroyed:
Beyond the Family Scars

*"For I am persuaded that neither death nor life, nor angels nor
principalities nor powers, nor things present nor things to come, nor
height nor depth, nor any other created thing, shall be able to
separate us from the love of God which is in Christ Jesus our Lord"
(Rom. 8:38–39 NKJV).*

Although suicide may be a part of your history, it doesn't have
to be part of your future. One of the most damaging consequences of
suicide is the message it seems to send to present and future generations that suicide is an acceptable coping mechanism for the family in
dealing with life's problems.

When a father kills himself following a job loss and facing potential financial ruin, he sends the message to his son that this life stress
is solved by suicide. Because the boy's mother is never able to process
her complicated feelings of rejection and abandonment, the son
grows up in an environment of isolation and confusion. He later has
difficulty maintaining stable relationships.

A grandfather, angry over presumed personal injustice, follows
the path of substance abuse and eventually suicide to deal with his
emotional pain. His daughter or son is plagued with a string of broken relationships and failed marriages precipitated by fear of rejection and abandonment.

A mother raised under the oppression of perfectionism grows

despondent over her perceived failures in life, buries her pain in stolen sips of alcohol, and one day swallows a lethal dose of pills along with her drink. Her little girl grows up wondering what she did to make her mother sad enough to kill herself. She later marries a verbally abusive and controlling man in her search for security and love. Her frustration increases daily as she tries to please her husband, and she begins to think suicide might be the only way out.

A teen sees his uncle kill himself over a failed love relationship. When the teen's girlfriend dumps him to go out with his best friend, he shoots the friend, his girlfriend, and himself in a fit of rage.

A young boy's father kills himself on a sunny summer afternoon. Years later, as the adult son approaches the age his father was when he died, he fears he will do the same thing out of some uncontrollable, overwhelming urge.

All of these are examples of the scars and debris left by suicide. The shifting fault line of a suicidal quake can go on for generations unless stilled by education and awareness.

Jeanna: From Scars to Stars—A Daughter's Story*

At age twenty, Jeanna is beautiful, poised, intelligent, and busy. As the reigning* Miss South Carolina, she lives a hectic life. With speaking appearances in up to four schools a day, as well as before church youth groups and civic organizations, Jeanna's Miss South Carolina cell phone and Day-Timer are always with her. To look at her radiant face, you would never guess the tragedy that lies in her past.

On September 13, 1999, Jeanna's phone rang. A college freshman, she was about to leave to teach an aerobics class on that Monday evening. Instead, she answered the phone. She recognized her father's voice, but he asked to speak to her roommate. She immediately sensed something was wrong. Her suspicion grew as her roommate's face turned red and she spoke only in a few monosyllables. When her

---

* Although Jeanna's year as Miss South Carolina has ended, she continues to promote awareness of and intervention for suicide and depression through several organizations.

roommate hung up the phone, the first words out of Jeanna's mouth were, "My mom's dead, isn't she? She killed herself." Her roommate's tears confirmed her suspicion. Jeanna says her first thought was a selfish one. "All I could think was, *For the rest of my life, people are going to feel sorry for me.*"

Several close friends immediately surrounded Jeanna. They waited with her while her pastor and youth minister made the almost two-hour trip to her college to transport her home. Jeanna's greatest concern following the news of her mother's suicide is one shared by all survivors—her mother's eternity. The myths and confusion surrounding suicide lead even Christians to question if suicide negates eternity in heaven.

Jeanna couldn't bring herself to pose the question to her pastor outright, so she simply asked, "What do you think about suicide?" The pastor perceived the unasked question within this query and wisely answered at that level. His ability to assure her that her mother's salvation was not jeopardized because of the act of suicide was her greatest comfort in those early hours of shock.

The circumstances leading up to Jeanna's mother's decision to kill herself began years before. While still in high school, Jeanna's mom was diagnosed with scoliosis, curvature of the spine. When Jeanna was in fifth grade, her mother's spinal curve was 36 degrees, but a fall resulted in a slipped disk, and her curve increased to 56 degrees. This increase in the curve was unusual and required surgery. Jeanna terms her mother's surgery as "barbaric." During the surgery metal rods were screwed into her spine and five vertebrae were fused together. Her mother's recovery took almost a year. During this time she was confined to a hospital bed at home. Overwhelmed by physical pain and feelings of helplessness, Jeanna's mom became depressed.

Jeanna recalls that for years following the surgery her mother was in pain, on pain medication, and constantly plagued with numerous health problems. Her mother fought valiantly to outrun the depression. Her faith in God helped her remain active and in good spirits. Once she was able, she became involved in church as Vacation Bible School director, taught Sunday school, and was a faithful choir member. At one point she served as interim minister of music. She was also a PTO officer and a loyal supporter at her children's various activities.

About a year before her suicide, Jeanna's mother began to struggle again with depression. She was facing additional surgery and was told that her back pain would never get better. Jeanna was a high school senior, her brother was about to marry, and Jeanna's parents would soon be empty-nesters.

&⅋ &⅋ &⅋

Jeanna recalled her mother's battle with depression and anxiety in the following interview:

Jeanna, is there a history of suicide in your family?

Yes. I really didn't put it all together until a month or so after my mother's death. It seems my mother's grandfather committed suicide. The details are sketchy, but apparently he either fell or jumped from a tree and was killed. Also, his daughter, my mother's aunt, committed suicide by jumping into a well. So my mother's death was a third-generation suicide.

Did you recognize any suicidal warning signs?

Now that I look back on it, I can see there were a lot of warning signs before my mother's suicide, but we didn't recognize them. She wasn't doing the things she normally did. She would sit all day, and when I came home, nothing would be done around the house—no laundry done, no plans for cooking supper, no housecleaning. I remember thinking sometimes that she was not a very good mother. She wouldn't go to the grocery store, and I didn't understand that. Later, I realized it was because she was having anxiety attacks. I believe that is what ultimately led to her decision to kill herself. She couldn't handle the anxiety attacks.

The summer before I went to college, I would wake up in the mornings to my mom pacing the floor and rubbing her hands together. She was very nervous.

Because mother didn't sleep well, she started sleeping on the sofa so she wouldn't keep my dad awake. She was taking medication for anxiety, and one night she took the whole bottle of pills. She was asleep on the sofa when I went to school and my dad went to work, but we didn't think anything about it because it really wasn't unusual for her to still be asleep when we left. My dad tried to call her during the day and couldn't get her. When he came home that night, she was still asleep on the sofa and everything in the house was just as it had been that morning. He took her to the hospital, and amazingly she survived.

She was admitted to the psychiatric ward and evaluated. She had depression, but I know she wasn't crazy. While she was in the hospital, her doctor took her off all the medication she was on, including her pain medication. The doctor put her on one drug that he said would take about twelve days to get into her system. After seven days, without telling my father my mother was suicidal, the doctor let her go home from the hospital. Two days later my mother killed herself. When the autopsy was performed, the new medication wasn't even in my mother's blood stream yet.

So your mother went from being on too much medication to none.

Yes. Perhaps if she had stayed in the hospital three more days before going home, she might have been OK.

Did your mother talk about feeling suicidal?

She really didn't live long enough for us to know anything.

In all the years of back pain, depression, and anxiety, did your mother ever say, "I wish I were dead"?

Oh, no, never. There was only one time in June before she died in September that I saw her have an anxiety attack, and I realized that she was probably not right mentally. I was eighteen years old and naïve, and I didn't realize that what she was experiencing was a chemical imbalance. We both cried that morning. I guess it was probably the first time she'd ever told anyone what she was feeling, and I could see for the first time how sick she was. That day she told me she didn't think she could stand it any more. That was the first time the thought ever crossed my mind, *What if she kills herself?* She immediately said, "Oh, no, I didn't mean that. I would never do anything to hurt you."

I believed her, and suicide never, ever entered my mind again until my dad called to say she was dead. I didn't even think suicide when she overdosed on pain medication and was in the psychiatric ward. I know it sounds so silly, but I just didn't think she would do it. She and I even made jokes while she was in the hospital about how it was so unnecessary for them to take everything away from her that she might use to hurt herself.

Looking back, do you think she was thinking about suicide?

I just don't think so, but she was a good actress. We lived with her, yet she was able to hide her real feelings from us. We didn't know what was going on in her mind. I don't blame her for what she did because I know she was in so much pain.

Tell me about the day she died.

It was a Monday, September 13, somewhere between 3:00 and 4:30 in the afternoon. My father called home and didn't get an answer. My grandmother, my mother's mother, lives across the street, so he called her and told her she had better check on my mother. So my grandmother is the one who found her. She called my father and said she thought she was dead. Mama shot herself. I can only imagine what it was like for my grandmother to find her like that.

Earlier that day my sister-in-law talked to my mother on the phone, and Mama told her to make a hair appointment for her later in the week. I really don't think she was planning to kill herself. The TV was on in the bedroom. I think she probably had a panic attack and didn't know what to do. She used a rifle that my father won at an insurance convention. The gun hadn't been fired since the 1970s and was in his closet.

Did your father experience guilt because she used that gun?

No, not really. I think my dad, my brother, and I were all realistic in the fact that we knew if Mama was determined to kill herself she was going to find some way to do it. She obviously tried with pills. If she hadn't used the gun, she would have drowned herself in our pool or slit her wrists or something else. I think if your loved one is suicidal you can't take the guilt on yourself because he or she will find some way to die, no matter what you do or don't do. You just can't blame yourself.

If I wanted to, I could look back on things I said to her and feel really guilty. All eighteen-year-olds say smart-aleck things to their parents. If I let myself, I could feel bad over things I said to her that probably didn't boost her self-esteem. I think we all have those moments even if it's not a suicide death. You can always think of things you wish you had said or done differently.

When did you last see your mother?

The day before she died. I had come home for the weekend. She had a different look on her face that weekend. She didn't go to church that Sunday because she didn't feel strong enough, but after church all of us ate lunch at my grandmother's house. My mother's eating habits were really strange, but that day she cleaned her plate. She sat in the floor, played with my baby cousin, and seemed really happy. We were all excited because we thought the medicine was really working. Either my mom thought she was getting better, or she already knew her time was almost up and had decided that was her last day. I went back to school that night. Before I left she hugged me. That was the last time I saw her.

What was it like to go home after her death?

Going into my house that night was really hard because there were so many people there. I felt like everyone was watching me and waiting to see my reaction. I hugged my brother first, and he was very emotional, and then my dad and he just had this whimper cry and said something like, "We're really in a mess." None of us ate for about three days.

The week after my mother died, I began researching depression and suicide. I wanted to try to understand what had happened. I didn't realize until then that depression is a mental illness.

I didn't want people to feel sorry for me, so I have felt the need to remain strong and be myself. That is how I have gotten through the healing process. I went through the stages of grief rather quickly. Of course, initially I was in shock. I had some of the strangest thoughts like, *My mother is never going to see me live out my dreams.*

Did the grief ever change for you? Did you become tearful?

Yes, eventually, but I had the support of my family and friends. I was raised in church, and my faith is strong. I felt I had the perfect life before this one tragedy happened to me. When I went back to college, I remember thinking, *I can't make it.* I just felt so weak and tired. I never really understood the power of prayer until that week after my mother's suicide. I felt the power of prayer so strongly, and I thought, *People all over the state are praying for me.* This helped me so much, and I got back to my normal routine. I knew sitting around feeling sorry for myself wasn't going to help me, so I pushed myself. It was hard. I can remember bursting into tears in ballet class, but I kept going.

Tell me about your mother's funeral? How did you get through it?

Well, my mom's funeral was awesome, if you can say that about a funeral. There were about eight hundred people there. The pastors who conducted the funeral shared humorous stories about my mother, and there was a lot of laughter. My mom was a very outgoing, fun-loving person before she got sick, so there were lots of fun stories. There was no mention of suicide. The pastor talked about life being made up of many moments and we shouldn't focus on the one weak moment she had when her life ended. He encouraged us not to let that moment overshadow all the wonderful moments she had for the other forty-three years of her life. To end the funeral we played a tape of my mom singing "He Never Failed Me Yet." I didn't want her funeral to be over. I enjoyed every minute of it. I didn't shed a tear. I felt a great sense of peace. The funeral was a celebration of my mom's life.

As part of my healing and recovery, I made a memory list of all the wonderful moments I remember having with my mother. I chose to focus on those moments rather than the difficult year before her death.

Another thing that helped me recover was meeting with a lady who has a daughter my age. Our families had a lot in common. This lady had bipolar disorder and had attempted suicide twice. She talked to my father, brother, and me. She told us why she tried to kill herself, what she was thinking, and how she felt. I was able to ask her lots of questions, and that really helped.

Your mother had been dying for a long time, hadn't she?

Yes, I think she had. Not only was she in a lot of physical pain; she was also dealing with a lot of mental pain. I can understand why she didn't want to live that way. Most people don't understand suicide, but when you've lived with that person, you may begin to understand why she did it. During the last year she didn't cook or clean. She stopped caring about her appearance and would go out of the house without even brushing her hair. I would think, *What is wrong with you!*

Were you maybe even a little relieved for her that her pain was over?

Yes.

Do you think she felt she was a burden?

She knew she was slowing us down, that her inability to function normally was a drain on the family.

Do you think she felt she was doing something good for her family?

Maybe. We will always have questions because she didn't leave a note, so we don't really know what she was thinking. I'm not sure I want to know what was going on in her mind during the last few minutes of her life.

Did you feel any anger toward the medical professionals who cared for your mother?

I was very angry. I wonder if things had been handled differently if she would still be alive. She might be in a wheelchair or a nursing home now, but we would still have her. It is sometimes hard for me to think about future events in my life like my wedding or having my first child and think what it will be like not having her with me. But I am very blessed to have my father because he is a better parent than some have with two parents. We have always been close, and my father has more faith than anyone I know. He set an example for me and my brother in the way he approached my mother's death and how he recovered. We looked at him and realized we could go on with our lives, too.

Do you worry about your dad or your brother becoming depressed or suicidal?

No, I really don't.

Your dad has done really well recovering.

Yes, very well.

Do you ever think he's done too well and maybe hasn't dealt with this totally?

Possibly.

Were you ever angry with God for your mother's death?

I really didn't experience anger at God. My father told me the night after she died that God never gives us anything we can't handle. I remember thinking, *This is definitely a test of that.* I'm sure my mother's suicide is the hardest thing I'll ever have to deal with. I had faith God could get me through, no matter how hard it was. I did experience some nervousness and fear in the months after my mother's death. I had a hard time being alone in the dorm room at night. I was scared, but I'm not really sure of what. I think I was afraid I would see a vision of my mother standing over me.

Did you experience any depression at all? Did you have problems eating or sleeping or crying a lot?

I really didn't cry much at all. People were concerned, but that is just my personality. I am more emotional now than I was before my mother's death, and this could be a good thing because I've softened and am not so tough skinned. There are days when a sad song will bring me to tears. Some days I don't think about my mother at all, and other days she's all I think about. I guess this is all a part of the healing process.

Have you had a hard time with the anniversary of her death, holidays, or birthdays?

Not really. The way I look at it, no particular day is harder than any other. There is always a sadness. However, the second Mother's Day after my mother's death was very hard for me. I went to church, and there was so much emphasis on mothers. It is still hard for me to see a mother and daughter together.

How about feelings of rejection and abandonment? Have you experienced any of those feelings?

Yes. I was really angry at times because I need my mother. *Didn't she realize I was going to need her?*

Have you ever experienced an unexpected sudden impact of your loss?

The first time we went out to eat together as a family after my mother's death was hard because I looked at the empty chair, and it hit me she wasn't there.

Jeanna, I think one of the things that helped you so much is being out-spoken about your experience with suicide. One of the mistakes I made was not talking about my father's death. It was fifteen years before I ever had any counseling or talked about what I was feeling.

I did experience some feelings of embarrassment because I didn't want people to think my mother was a freak or a psycho. I thought it would change people's perception of me and my family to know my mother killed herself. There is still so much stigma. Suicide seems to lower people's respect for a family. I was really embarrassed to have to tell people who didn't know me. One of my professors asked how my mom died, and I didn't even answer her. I didn't want to tell her. Now I can talk about her suicide.

What do you say now when someone asks that question?

I'm able to say, "She killed herself," or, "She committed suicide."

Those words are hard to say, aren't they?

Yes. Every time I have to tell someone, I'm always wondering what they are thinking. The stigma is there. But I usually try to give a little of the story to help them understand how sick she was.

Did you have concerns about your mom's eternity?

Yes, initially. One of the first things I said to my friend after I heard about my mother's death was, "I guess this means my mama is in hell." She said, "No, Jeanna, your mother loved the Lord, and she's in heaven." But I doubted her. Then when I asked my pastor what he thought about suicide on the ride home, he told me not accepting Jesus is the only unpardonable sin and assured me that my mother was in heaven because she had accepted Jesus. I believe that, and I've never questioned again.

Your choice of suicide awareness as your platform is a wonderful way to memorialize your mother. If you could talk to her again, what would you tell her?

I don't know if I would ask her what was going on in her head the day she killed herself or if I would tell her about this year, about winning the Miss South Carolina crown.

What are your personal goals?

I want to be a professional photographer. But even after I give up my crown, I'll still have my story to tell. Forever I'll be a spokesperson for suicide awareness and intervention. The national Mental Health Association is interested in having me as a spokesperson. I think a lot of doors I don't even know about yet will open for me. Obviously, if I can help other people, I will. I've partnered with the Jason Foundation to get the materials I need for handouts in speaking at schools.

You seem to have a passion for speaking about your platform.

I have the personal connection, and, yes, I believe I was destined to speak about suicide.

Suicide affects 85 percent of the population in some way, but it still isn't talked about. People think they are alone and the only ones to have gone through it, and you can let them know that is not the case.

The first time I spoke at a high school, I was nervous because I didn't know how the students would react. In the first classroom the teacher told me two of the students had attempted suicide. In the next room the father of one of the students had killed himself. Within the first hour I encountered three people affected by suicide.

After I spoke to a service organization, an eighty-five-year-old man told me his grandfather committed suicide. I spoke in one county where there were four teen suicides over the summer. So it doesn't matter what age you are; almost everyone has been affected by suicide.

God is using for good what happened to you. You'll never know until you get to heaven how many lives you touched because of your mom's suicide. That is probably the only redeeming factor in the loss of your mother.

I choose not to focus on the circumstances of my mother's death. I decided I couldn't do anything about her death, so I may as well turn it into something positive.

That is an unusual way to approach it because many survivors slip into a pattern of depression and suicidal thoughts themselves.

So many people have shared with me their own struggle with depression. This helped me realize what a big problem depression is. I really feel a burden to do something to make people aware how much of an epidemic depression and suicide are.

Is there any Bible verse that has been special to you in your recovery?

Romans 13:12: "The night is nearly over; the day is almost here. So let us put aside the deeds of darkness and put on the armor of light." When I read that verse, I think all the horribleness and darkness regarding my mother's depression and death is over and something awesome is about to happen. I use this verse to challenge people to turn the negative things in life into positives.

Jeanna, your mom would be very proud of you.

k k k

ANOTHER DAUGHTER'S STORY

"My mother tried to kill herself once."

Holly's statement dropped like a bomb into the casual dinner conversation. Her voice took on a detached quality and melted to almost a whisper. The other four at the table made fleeting eye contact as one asked, "How old were you?"

"I'm not sure," replied Holly with a tiny smile. "I've blocked it out. About eight or nine, I think. I don't remember the season of the year, but it was a Sunday. We went to church, but mother stayed home because she hadn't been feeling well. She was in her gown when we left."

"During the service the Lord gave me a vision. I saw my mother lying on the floor, dressed, in a certain position, and I knew she had done it. I wanted to tell Daddy we should go home, but I knew he would think I was crazy. When we got home, I made sure I was the first one in the house. I found her. She was lying in exactly the same position and was wearing the same clothes I had seen in the vision."

"Did she take pills?" someone asked.

"No, she shot herself in the chest. It's a wonder she didn't hit her heart. I even knew it was a chest wound before I saw her. In the vision I clearly saw the blood on her chest. No one ever believed me about the vision, but I think God allowed me to have it to prepare me."

This is Holly's story about her mother.

"She struggles with depression and has lots of physical ailments. There is a history of suicide and mental illness in her family. My mother is bipolar. Her mother was committed to a psychiatric hospital when mother was preschool age. She never came home. I think mother learned as a child that she could get attention by being sick. Even today she loves the attention she gets from having crises in her life.

"Just recently I found out mother lied to me about her suicide attempt. She always told me she did it to escape her physical pain, but she wasn't really trying to commit suicide. I have learned in the past few years that she left a suicide note. I've never seen the note, but one of my siblings told me it exists.

"My siblings and I have talked recently about how Mother's suicide attempt changed how we related to her. We tiptoed around her emotions after the attempt. There are things children and teenagers usually complain about or beg for, but we never did for fear of upsetting her and maybe causing her to try to kill herself again. When I look back, I see we all lived with a great deal of fear. There was never any attempt to provide counseling for my siblings or me, nor did my parents have any. This was a traumatic event for our family, but it was never discussed—ever.

"Quite honestly, there were many times since Mother's suicide attempt that I have wished she had been successful because living with the fear of her doing it again has been so hard. But I am also thankful she didn't succeed because I know I would have had such guilt for not telling Daddy in church we should go home to check on her.

"I think mother's suicide attempt changed the way my siblings and I related to one another and to my parents and the way my parents related to each other and to us. It basically changed everything.

We lost any chance at family closeness and connection. From the outside, we appeared to be a normal, happy family, but I felt my whole childhood was built around secrets.

"It was also hard for me because from an early age I was forced to take on the 'mother' role in the family. Mother was not able to do much for a while, and I was responsible for cooking and cleaning. I had to grow up very fast. Even today I feel I am the mother in the relationship and she is like a child.

"As a child, I cried myself to sleep every night praying for her emotional healing. I've spent a lot of time over the years wondering if Mother would try to kill herself again or if I had done something to cause her attempt. Finally, I just got to the point that I realized if she did I couldn't stop it. It would be her decision.

"Personally, one of the greatest effects Mother's suicide attempt had on me was to make me think I had to be 'Little Miss Perfect' so she wouldn't do it again. After I had children, I realized I was imposing expectations of perfectionism on them. I've had to work hard to break out of that and realize we don't have to be perfect. The Beth Moore Bible Study *Breaking Free* has helped me to break the cycle of repeating some detrimental patterns with my children.

"Another way my mother's suicide attempt has affected me is it has made me a very nonconfrontational person. I was always afraid to cross her because it might upset her enough to cause her to try to kill herself. I remember talking back to her once. She just turned and left the house. One of my siblings screamed at me for doing that, and it was then I realized we were all living in fear of what she might do. I guess there was fear on this occasion that I had verbally loaded and handed her a gun. We were both afraid she would kill herself and we would never see her again.

"Another thing I struggle with is control issues. I couldn't control my circumstances as a child, so as an adult I began to control my environment. I have to have everything around me orderly. I feel I can't stand it if my house is messy.

"Several years ago I realized I needed counseling. Everyone tells me how much I look like my mother, and there is a strong resemblance, but I resent people telling me that. I don't want to be identified with her just because we favor physically. I'm not my mother. I am a very different person inside.

"Through counseling I was able to see that although I may look like her, I am not her, and I'm not going to do what she did. I'm not going to try to kill myself. But it is a cloud that hangs over me. For years Mother has said, 'Just wait, you'll get depressed, and then you'll understand about killing yourself.' I don't need to hear that. I'm not going to do what she did. I realize now she has always emotionally abused me to get me to do what she wants. I constantly deal with feelings of guilt because I can't make my mother happy. No matter what I do, it will never be enough because her unhappiness comes from within.

"In the past few years, I've started to realize I have to live my life to please God, not my mother. I have spent a large portion of my life trying to please her, but it is something that will never happen. I understand now I can't please her and I can't change her. If she chooses to be sad and depressed, I have to let her. I don't have the ability to make things different for her. She has to be the one to do that. I can pray for her, and I can see to her physical comfort, but I am not responsible for her emotional health. I have to remind myself of this constantly. It is only through a day-by-day walk with God that I can function.

"My mother is a master at emotional abuse. She knows just what to say and do to cause me to feel guilty. Sometimes I think, *How many times am I supposed to forgive her for this?* Then God reminds me that I should forgive her every time. Many times I let my mother rob me of joy. Growing up, there was no joy and laughter in my home. That is different for me now. God has given me a husband, a son, and a daughter who make me laugh! Jesus came to set the captives free and bring hope. Because of the freedom I enjoy in Christ, I don't have to dread my life or feel I might become depressed like my mother.

"Many times I wish I didn't have to deal with my mother at all. I wonder what my life would be like. When mother dies, I think what

I will regret most is not what I've lost but what I never had in the way of a healthy mother-daughter relationship."

&8 &8 &8

The stories of these two daughters are similar in some ways, yet vastly different. The daughter whose mother is dead, can talk about her mother's death and the circumstances. Her mother's suicide is literally a platform to allow her to move on with her life and encourage and aid other survivors. The scars of suicide have given her maturity and depth and have launched her forward in her healing and recovery.

The other daughter's story is more often reality. The nature of her surviving, of living with her mother's ongoing potential for suicide, has caused her to be more inward than outward. She can't talk about the shadow of suicide on her life or reveal her identity because she continues to interact daily or weekly with a parent who attempted suicide. There is always the nagging worry that perhaps there may be other attempts. Emotional issues and fears continue to plague the relationship. Resolution, restoration, and rebuilding are elusive. Her survival story is ongoing. Yet she has coped through her faith in Jesus Christ and her belief in the power of the Holy Spirit to break the bondage of the past.

AFTERGLOW

1. Take steps now to break the legacy of suicide for your family.

2. Make a list of all the positive qualities of your deceased loved one.

3. Make a list of the positive contributions of your family spanning several generations.

CHAPTER 6

Picking Up the Pieces:
Deciding to Rebuild

"[You] will rebuild the ancient ruins and will raise up the age-old foundations; you will be called Repairer of Broken Walls, Restorer of Streets with Dwellings" (Isa. 58:12).

The secondary effects of an earthquake are often greater than the actual event: fires from broken gas mains, flooding from ruptured water lines, theft and looting in unprotected areas, and panic and fear as aftershocks continue. Connections of all kinds are broken, including communications. In a matter of minutes, everything that is stable and firm is destroyed. Once-familiar surroundings, now devastated, are oddly unrecognizable.

Just as earthquake survivors must sift through the debris of their homes and lives, so suicide survivors must deal with the emotional and practical fallout that remains. Life becomes unstable and uncertain. It is possible to rebuild your life following suicide, but it involves hard, painstaking work.

When a city is rebuilt following an earthquake, many times it takes on a totally new look. Older structures previously in need of renewal are leveled, and new buildings arise in their place. Architecturally, these structures are stronger and more stable, correcting interior and exterior design problems.

Structures that weather quakes are those with deep, firm foundations. Those left standing often sustain cracks, which threaten their stability now or in later years. These areas of weakness must be addressed in order to prevent future damage.

In 1886, Charleston, South Carolina, sustained one of the largest earthquakes ever recorded on the east coast. Its epicenter was twenty-five miles northwest of the city in Summerville. Shocks were felt as far away as Canada. As a result of this quake, hundreds of buildings were structurally damaged or destroyed. Some were repaired or rebuilt using long iron rods for reinforcement. Iron rods were run through walls and anchored with a large washer-type device called a "gib plate" and an iron nut. These are in evidence on many buildings in Charleston today and are commonly known as "earthquake bolts." Because these earthquake bolts were plain and owners felt them unattractive, many chose to disguise them with cast iron decorations such as lions' heads, stars, or ornate medallions.

Whether your life was leveled by the effects of suicide or only sustained structural cracks, you have the option to rebuild your life differently and better. You can choose to address issues that are difficult to face, knowing your life will be more stable following the process. You may need to piece your life back together with "earthquake bolts." Your earthquake bolt may be your ability to keep a sense of humor or to become the encourager for your family in spite of your loss. Your leadership in addressing the practical matters of insurance claims or probation of the will may be the lion's head medallion that holds life together. Your earthquake bolt may be a daily infusion of God's Word as a reminder of his faithfulness in this life-shattering event.

Your choice of a victor's mentality rather than a victim's mentality is crucial in the rebuilding process. Many suicide survivors succumb to a victim's mode of thinking and tend to wallow in their pain, perhaps for the rest of their lives. Just as an earthquake survivor would not choose to live in a tent city amid the rubble when there is the option of rebuilding and living in a new house, so you must decide to move from your devastation. Many times an earthquake survivor rebuilds on the same site. Moving on with your life doesn't necessarily mean escaping or moving away. A firm foundation can be salvaged. Allow Jesus to be that firm foundation as you rebuild your life.

No city damaged by an earthquake or any other disaster leaves the debris and lives in it from then on. Many times cleanup begins almost immediately—that day or the next. This was evidenced in New York City following the World Trade Center collapse and at the Pentagon in Washington, D.C., on September 11, 2001. Although the cleanup task was mammoth and lives were crushed by grief, work began almost immediately. Rescue workers searched for protected pockets of survivors and in many cases were rewarded for their efforts. Every life they saved was precious. In spite of fear of future acts of terrorism, rescue work and rubble removal continued for months with a goal of completion within a year's time.

A year is a realistic goal for your rubble removal, but don't consider it failure if initial recovery takes longer. Healing and recovery are very much individualized. Focus on the "survivor" aspect of your designation of suicide survivor, and work hard to avoid becoming stuck in "frozen" grief.

GRIEVING THE LOSS

Because suicide is such an emotional explosion, suicide survivors may become stuck at one or more stages of grief, and some may indeed become frozen in their grief. In *After Suicide,* John H. Hewitt cites "shrine building" as a certain path to frozen grief. Hewitt says, "This drive toward creating a 'museum to the deceased' is one way to ensure a lifetime of grief. Visiting the grave every day may be helpful for a while, but it can soon become your method of refusing to let go. . . . Another method of shrine-building is the preservation of a room in the house 'just like it was when he died.' This is 'frozen' grief. It promises a lifetime of mourning for those who succumb to its nostalgic temptations."[6]

In speaking of grief in "After a Suicide," Randy Christian says, "The awkwardness of grief tempts us to hide from the truth. Those bereaved by suicide are tempted to avoid the painful fact that a loved one took his or her life. But hiding the fact only makes it harder to recover from the grief."[7]

It is unrealistic to expect any grief to be an orderly process. Grief often appears to be a two-steps-forward, one-step-back progression. It is the very nature of suicide grief to be acute and traumatic. No matter how well you think you are doing, expect setbacks. The ebb and flow of emotion lends itself to discovery of unresolved pockets of grief. You may uncover a gaping hole just when you think the wound is almost healed.

Don't allow yourself to become discouraged when this happens. Call a trusted friend and discuss what you are experiencing, even if you think the person is tired of hearing you talk about your grief. Talking about your pain is an effective method of healing. James 5:16 speaks of confession of sins and prayer as a path to healing. Likewise, admitting anger and acknowledging your grief, coupled with prayer, is a godly formula for healing.

In some ways emotional pain is like a child with a fresh wound. He immediately clamps his hand over the wound and doesn't want to show it to anyone for fear that it is worse than he thinks or that the first aid will be painful. When a child has a bad scrape, the wound is often filled with gravel or dirt. It is necessary to clean out the debris even if the first aid stings and is painful or uncomfortable. If the wound is not cleansed, it will never heal properly. It is the same with suicide survivor recovery.

When emotional pain is so great, you don't want anyone else to look at it until several months later. But if you don't follow through with processing the complicated emotions surrounding suicide, healing will never be complete. I encourage counselees to work through the pain and not leave things half done because eventually some remnant of emotional pain will return with greater intensity. As with most other things in life, a dreaded task, once initiated, must be carried through to completion. Like remodeling your home or cleaning out the garage, you have to be willing to live in a mess for a while in order to complete the task.

In January 1979, I did a ministerial apprenticeship at Binkley Baptist Church in Chapel Hill, North Carolina. As part of that apprenticeship, I shadowed a chaplain in the burn unit of North Carolina Memorial Hospital (now UNC Hospital). Burn patients undergo great physical trauma. When a severe burn occurs, the nerves are burned as well as the skin. Because the nerve endings are destroyed, the patients feel no pain immediately after being burned. Patients first feel pain when the burn begins to heal. First and second-degree burns will usually heal on their own. Third-degree burns require the intervention of skin grafts.

Often, if death occurs in a multitrauma patient, it comes by way of something unrelated to the initial trauma—something that seems almost insignificant in light of the other injuries, like pneumonia or infection. Because the patient's immune system is so weakened by the trauma, a "small thing" can lead to death.

After a suicide, "emotional immunities" are weakened as well, and survivors are more susceptible to the small things. A bad day at work, a financial setback, a fender bender, or a quarrel with a loved one—something that is an everyday part of life and is easily handled under normal circumstances—can trigger a downward spiral for a suicide survivor.

As with a severe burn patient, a suicide survivor experiences an emotional third-degree burn. At first the person is in shock. Later the person begins to experience the full depth of the emotional pain. Suicide is a multisystem trauma to the survivor.

In many ways the grieving process for suicide survivors is similar to that for those experiencing any kind of loss. You can expect to go through the normal passages of the grieving process. Grieving is the healing of an emotional wound just as a scab is the way the body heals a flesh wound. Grief allows a person to acknowledge a loss and then look forward to what's next in life. Grieving is a process which sometimes takes months or years. The process shouldn't be rushed in order to get through it. Each individual grieves in a unique way.

Trying to model your particular grief process after someone else's is not a good idea. Don't let someone convince you that you should be "over" the grief in a certain time frame. The grief process shouldn't be rushed, but it can be postponed. But no matter how long you delay, the grief will wait for you. At some point you will have to grieve the loss.

Often when grief is discussed, clinical words like *shock, denial, bargaining,* and *catharsis* are used. These terms can be hard for some people to understand. I've always been more comfortable with describing the grieving process as *sad, mad, glad.*

Initially persons in the grieving process feel loss, emptiness, and sadness. They may feel numb or cry and want to be left alone. In most cases anger comes later. As with physical injury, the deeper feelings and emotions may not appear until days or even months later.

When grieving people enter the *mad* stage, they tend to cry less, talk more, and want to seek retribution for their loss. It is in this phase that survivors begin to voice intentions of suing doctors, rant against the ineffectiveness of medications, or crusade against handguns. During this stage of grieving, individuals are probably the most emotionally out of control. Their agitation may even cause them to feel worse than they did immediately after the death of their loved one.

Because the stages of grief are cyclical and incremental rather than linear, it is not uncommon for people to vacillate between the various stages.

The goal of the grief process is to reach *glad.* Although this word seems ill-fitting with regard to grief, it means arriving at a place where you can give thanks in your pain, as opposed to being glad for your loved one's death. *Glad* indicates a return to normal, although a new normal. *Glad* is finding joy and happiness in aspects of life apart from the grief.

The good news is that the pain of grief will lessen in time. You will gradually become aware that you have gone hours or days without thinking of your loss. A time of loss can often be the time of greatest growth in your life. Just as you experienced physical growing pains as a child, the emotional and spiritual growth you gain because of your loss will be painful. Make the choice to learn and grow through the pain rather than running from it.

THE SUPPORT GROUP: BRIDGE TO RECOVERY

A good way to begin to rebuild your life is to join or start a suicide survivors' support group. Often your local mental health association or churches in your city will have information about groups already in existence. Being a member of a group does several things. It provides a safe place to discuss what you are thinking and feeling with other people who understand your unique pain. A support group also helps you to realize you are not the only one going through the complex emotional process of healing from suicide.

Many people view a support group as a crutch for the emotionally weak. We all have emotional weaknesses and needs, whether we are willing to admit them or not. From my experience, those involved in a support group are some of the most emotionally healthy people I know. It takes a strong person to agree to go to a support group. Don't let fear of exposing yourself emotionally in front of a group of people you don't know stop you from going. You may find that there is at least one person in the group with whom you can identify. That connection will draw you into the group and keep you coming back.

Once you have become more at ease in the group, continue to participate. You may feel the group has heard it all, but the members of the group and the dynamics of the group are constantly changing. Remember, when you are feeling better, there is someone there for the first time who is where you were three or six months ago or two years ago. You may be that one person with whom a newcomer connects. Your presence in the group is valuable, no matter how long you have been attending.

One of the best meetings our suicide survivors' support group had was the night I declared no one could say anything sad or negative. For the next hour the members told one humorous story after another about their loved ones. That night, laughter truly was our best medicine. "A cheerful heart is good medicine, but a crushed spirit dries up the bones" (Prov. 17:22).

Another View of the Support Group: An Outsider Looking In (Candy Visits the Group)

I arrived early for the monthly meeting of the Survivors of Suicide support group at a local church. My plan was to find a seat in the corner and blend into the wall. But the group members had other ideas. Several people introduced themselves and then waited patiently for my story. Even though my reason for being there was not what they expected, I was immediately made to feel welcome.

As I looked around the room at the faces of those present (ten women, three men), I realized they were just like me. Although I don't have the suicide connection, I could relate to their sense of loss from my own personal experiences. They are a unique community of pain—but then, don't we all need love, encouragement, and support at times in our lives?

The meeting format was informal and open. Their first item of business was discussion about a quarterly newsletter. Members were encouraged to submit poems and articles written by survivors as well as loved ones who had attempted or committed suicide. One member mentioned the therapeutic benefits of writing. There was also discussion of updating a current group list and a request for those willing to be "on call" for members who were having a hard time dealing with their loss. The "on call" list would include mention of the loved one lost, i.e., son, husband, daughter, etc. so the person in need could choose someone from the list with a similar loss. A member encouraged the newcomers not to feel they had to be strong. "We all need someone to cry with once in a while."

I guess I was a little surprised when the discussion moved to the location and time for the group's annual Christmas party. Why I expected this group to be incapable of celebration, I don't know. The mood of the group noticeably lightened during this portion of the meeting. One member did mention that last year's Christmas party was too difficult and sent her on a downward spiral for several months. Her difficulty was not the party itself but the memories of other Christmases before her loved one's death.

The room floated in silence for several minutes. I found myself uncomfortable with the change. There was noticeable shuffling and shifting, but still no one spoke. Finally, the facilitator, an associate pastor at the church, broke the silence with a few wise words about grief. "Grief makes us feel like we want to escape and go away. There is always going to be something or some date to remind you of your loss. It's not easy to do, but facing the grief is the best way to handle it."

His words hung in the air briefly before someone else spoke. The comments came slowly at first but then increased. One spoke of going to the wedding of the sister of a lost loved one, stating that she was able to actually enjoy herself even though there were difficult moments. She was affirmed by one who sat cross-legged on the floor, "That was a major step for you. That was huge." Others around the room nodded their agreement.

Another member of the group said she had always been told she would feel better in a year. "It didn't get easier after a year." Someone else mentioned how you want to hurry the process along but can't. Others said they didn't feel better for at least two years. One lady quietly referred to grieving the loss of her son as a gradual process. "After three years I sometimes wonder if I'm really better, but then I remember how I felt after it first happened, and I know I've made progress. My recovery has been very gradual."

From across the room came the comment, "After five years it's still hard, but you adjust and you feel better and learn to enjoy the memories. The pain is so intense at first that it has to get better or you couldn't take it. I don't think you could live with that level of emotional pain for long."

Another lady, new to the group, spoke of sitting beside a teenager at a football game who reminded her strongly of her dead son. "I just enjoyed the afternoon. There were so many things about that kid that reminded me of my son. As we were leaving, I thought, *Thanks for giving me another afternoon with my son.*" At this point the facilitator spoke of being thankful for small gifts. He said survivors often search out someone or something familiar that reminds them of their loved one.

The same lady spoke of having people treat her like she had a contagious disease or cancer when they learn her son committed suicide. She said it makes her feel strange to have people look at her funny and back off when the word *suicide* is mentioned. "People don't talk to you because they are afraid they will make you cry.

Sometimes I wish they would just ask me how I'm feeling. It's OK if it makes me cry to talk about it."

Her comments really caused me to think. Perhaps, until now, I've been one of those who backed off at the mention of suicide. It helped me see anew how much suicide survivors suffer. Not just from the emotional pain of the loss but from how society views and treats them once suicide enters their lives. It makes me want to encourage others even more to pray and come alongside those who are grieving a suicide loss.

The discussion turned abruptly to the events of September 11, 2001, and the emotional upheaval the terrorist attacks precipitated for these survivors. Several stated that they identified so closely with the families of the victims because without warning these families lost loved ones. Someone mentioned a difference: our loved ones wanted to die; the victims of September 11 didn't want to die. Others talked about not being able to tear themselves from the television for days and of the return of torrents of tears. "Those first few days were very, very hard for me because I felt the return of the suicide pain very intensely," commented another. "September 11 plunged our nation into an intense state of grief," spoke the facilitator.

The discussion took another turn at this point. Several talked about how difficult it is to lose contact with the friends of their dead children. "At first my son's friends still came by the house, but gradually they quit coming. That has been hard for me. It feels like you lose another part of your child." Another said her son's friend came by to show her his new truck. "I knew he wanted to be showing his truck to my son, but it made me feel good that he was there showing it to me. This same friend asked for a copy of the suicide note because he is mentioned in it."

There were a few interesting thoughts on signs in nature that help grieving and recovery and talk of how some people feel closer to loved ones in certain locations, usually outside. One person mentioned being encircled by a whirlwind of leaves during a period of intense grief for her loved one and seeing that as a sign to move on with her life.

Following this, the facilitator brought the meeting to a close as everyone stood, held hands, and the meeting was closed with prayer. Many lingered to talk. Several people approached me, thanked me for being there, and encouraged me to return. One woman explained her connection to three others at the meeting, all grieving the loss of the same loved one. "My husband just can't make himself come to the meetings" confided one lady. "He says he gets too emotional. But he supports the group in other ways." Indeed, during the course of the meeting, I learned of several who make practical contributions to the group. One made the arrangements for the Christmas party. Another printed the newsletter.

As I left the room, I heard several members making plans to get together outside the regular group time. The hubbub was punctuated with occasional laughter. Life goes on.

How to Start a Survivors of Suicide (S.O.S) Group

You met Larry in chapter 2. A veteran in starting suicide survivor groups, he offers the following advice:

- Contact local pastors and/or the mental health association.
- Solicit financial support. This usually involves only a small amount necessary for mailings, newsletters, and brochures. A church, funeral home, or mental health association may be willing to underwrite group expenses.
- Get the word out through local media—radio, television, and newspaper.
- Distribute brochures about the group to various locations, including mortuaries, cemeteries, hospitals, churches, and emergency medical personnel. Include information about the meeting time, date, location, and contact phone numbers. Mention that the meetings are free of charge.
- Arrange to have a trained counselor facilitate the meetings. It is important to have a counselor who can follow up with members.
- Use a free-form program, "self-help" format.

- It is fine to schedule speakers from time to time, but remember this limits the amount of time open for discussion. Talking about their pain is what suicide survivors need most.
- Once the group is organized, consider publishing a quarterly newsletter. You may want to form a committee for this purpose.
- Provide each member with a group roster and have someone be responsible for mailing monthly meeting notices.

Starting Survivors of Suicide (S.O.S) groups has played a major role in helping Larry heal from the deaths in his family. He views helping others by means of the group as a way to bring his tragedy full circle. It can be the same for you. If there is no survivors' group in your community, get one started. Pray about being the one to form a group to meet the deep needs of others in your community.

SIFTING THE RUBBLE: DISCOVERING INTACT TREASURES

Pleasant memories of lost loved ones are like pearls amid a sea of pain and confusion. As an earthquake survivor might clutch a treasured possession found among the rubble, so treasured memories are precious amid the reality of the present for suicide survivors. Perhaps your pearl is a favorite place you enjoyed being with your loved one. Or maybe it is carrying on a project she began but never completed. Sift the rubble to discover your treasure, and allow it to be a bright spot in your recovery.

JACK'S STORY

Jack is a neat little man with a personality as engaging as his smile. He enjoys rising with the dawn so he won't miss anything. "I look forward to every day," he states with confidence. This sunny outlook on life is in direct opposition to the thunderous quake of suicide that exploded into Jack's life with the death of his son, Eric.

As Jack relayed the account of Eric's life and death, the only hint of the deep emotion he still experiences was a twitch of his mustache and a slight misting of his eyes.

As is the case with many suicides, Eric suffered chronic health problems and relationship struggles. Both figure heavily in the equation of the suicidal mind-set. Eric's kidney disease was discovered when he was only nine years old. Jack, an avid golfer, had already taught his son the game. Eric had his first kidney stone attack while playing golf with dad. Eric fainted and was rushed to the doctor. Later that day he had surgery. Thus began his initiation into the painful journey of surgeries and treatments for a condition that caused his body to produce over one hundred kidney stones during his thirty-six years of life. By the time Eric took his own life, he was going for monthly lithotripsy treatments, facing a never-ending succession of doctor visits, and was addicted to pain-killing drugs.

Eric's goal of joining the Air Force like his father before him went unrealized as he failed to pass the entrance physical because of his kidney condition. Further discouragement ensued when Eric was forced to go on permanent disability from his job.

The disappointment of one failed marriage and the inability to have children in a second marriage hastened Eric's downward spiral. In the days leading up to his death, Eric and his wife argued. Perhaps he feared the end of this relationship also. He spent one night in a motel before staying the second night at his mother's house. On Monday morning his mother went on a day long business trip and left Eric sleeping. She returned that night to find him dead, having run a hose from his exhaust pipe to the inside of the car and dying of carbon monoxide poisoning.

Jack's ability to remain upbeat and forward-looking in spite of Eric's death revolves around several things. "I know I'm going to see him again one day in heaven," Jack states with a smile, "and I cherish my memories of Eric. There are certain places I go where I feel his presence. I feel close to him there. I think Eric's mother struggles with guilt, feeling if she had been at home that day, she could have prevented him from killing himself. I think he had made up his mind. If he hadn't done it that day, he would have done it eventually. I have to focus on the good memories."

Several special memories helped Jack make the transition to life without Eric. The first is something that occurred a few days before Eric's suicide. Jack was playing golf in a foursome. When they got to the eighth hole, Eric drove up and offered to give his dad a ride up the hill. Jack took him up on his offer. As they headed up the hill, Eric yelled to the other three players, "My dad's going to birdie this hole!" Jack did. As Jack teed up for the ninth hole, Eric said he needed to get to his part-time job in the pro shop. Jack encouraged him to stay a while longer. "Don't go yet. Don't leave me now, son. You're my good luck charm. If you stay, I'll birdie this hole, too." Eric stayed with his dad, and Jack birdied the next two holes. Eric insisted he was late for work at the eleventh hole. Jack and Eric parted with an "I love you. See you soon." That was the last time Jack saw Eric.

"I couldn't look at him in the casket," Jack said. "I wanted to remember him the way he was that day on the golf course. Every time I get to the eighth hole I feel his presence. I feel him there more than any other place. Recently I felt as if he met me there. It was almost as if I heard him say, 'Let me putt it, Dad.' I sank the putt, and I couldn't help smiling."

"The other thing that got me through the pain of Eric's suicide happened the Sunday after his death. I was to teach a new Sunday school class at my daughter's church. When I got in the building, I realized I had left my Bible in the car. When I went back to get it, my Bible was open in the front passenger seat with a copy of Eric's obituary lying across it. I hadn't left it that way, but I took comfort in finding it there like that. I felt Eric was saying, 'Dad, I'm here, too.'"

Jack says he reflects often on those two incidents. The note Eric left his dad when he killed himself read, "Remember Dad, I love you, and I'll always be with you." Jack knows this is true, although he says nothing ever hurt him worse than Eric's suicide. He believes if Eric had asked himself one question he would never have taken his own life. That question is: How will this affect my family? "I think there is a complete mental breakdown for the person who commits suicide. That person isn't living in reality and can't think how his actions will affect others. No matter how dark things appear, there is always light at the end of the tunnel, but the suicidal person can't even see a glimmer."

Although Jack has leaned heavily on pleasant memories to aid in his recovery, he also joined a support group. "I've been a member of the support group for about two years," he says. The support group meetings are something Jack looks forward to. He says they help him put his pain in perspective. "No matter how bad things are in my life, there is always someone who has it worse. If I can go to the group and be an encouragement to someone there, it helps me feel better."

"You have to go on and live your life, but suicide is something you can't forget. It helps me to think I'm only going to miss Eric for a little while and then we'll be reunited. You have to have faith. It carries you through."

MEMORIALIZE YOUR LOVED ONE

Finding a way to remember your loved one in a positive way can speed the recovery process. One way to do this is to make a contribution in memory of your loved one. Although you can't bring him or her back, you can do something to help others. Making a contribution will cause you to turn outward and heighten your awareness of other hurting people. Select a charity that has meaning for you or your loved one, or make a contribution to a church building fund.

Remembering the anniversary of the suicide is another way to memorialize the person you have lost. I used to dread the anniversary of my father's death, but over the years the sense of dread has lessened. I encourage survivors to take the day off from work and do something fun. Try to engage in a positive activity on that day. Don't make it a day to be downcast and sorrowful. Sometimes I choose to make the anniversary of my father's death a day of fasting and prayer. Perhaps more than any other day of the year, on that day I need to focus on God and receive a blessing from him.

AFTERGLOW

1. Determine if there is an S.O.S. group in your community. If not, prayerfully consider starting one.

2. Focus on your status as a "survivor," and practice having a victor's mentality.

3. Recall a favorite memory of your loved one, and record it in a journal or on tape.

4. Think of your own personal way to memorialize your loved one.

"For I know the plans I have for you," declares the LORD, *"plans to prosper you and not to harm you, plans to give you hope and a future" (Jer. 29:11).*

CHAPTER 7

❧

Understanding Seismic Indicators:
Suicide Intervention

"Don't harm yourself! We are all here!" (Acts 16:28).

For years I have wanted to see the body of Christ equipped with the necessary skills to recognize and intervene in the lives of suicidal individuals. My doctoral thesis spoke to this issue. I am firmly convinced that with education and awareness many suicides could be prevented.

Acts 16:25–34 contains an account of a successful suicide intervention. Paul and Silas, imprisoned for casting out a spirit from a slave girl, were having a midnight prayer meeting. Suddenly a violent earthquake shook the foundation of the prison. The cell doors flew open, and everyone's chains were loosed. The Philippian jailer, fearing his prisoners had escaped, drew his sword to kill himself. Paul intervened by shouting, "Don't harm yourself! We are all here!"

Common sense indicates that Paul and Silas should have fled the destroyed jail to prevent recapture. In an earthquake the obvious thing to do would have been to run for their lives. But the obvious is not always the right thing. Paul, realizing the jailer was about to take his own life, quickly prevented the man's suicide. Paul saw the need and took immediate action. In this rare case an earthquake was a good thing. The powerful mixture of prayer and praise led to an event with far-reaching consequences. In the wake of the earthquake, a suicide was prevented, and a life change occurred.

Not only did Paul save the jailer's life physically; he also saved his life spiritually. The jailer fell trembling before Paul and Silas and asked, "Men, what must I do to be saved?" He replied, "Believe in the Lord Jesus, and you will be saved—you and your household" (v. 31). The effects of Paul's intervention saved not only the jailer but his family as well. Salvation is intended to be and can be a family experience.

Unfortunately, unlike Paul, most people live in a state of denial regarding suicidal tendencies in themselves and others. This denial doesn't always stem from indifference but rather from lack of information. Many of us are taught avoidance of life issues, such as unresolved conflict, anger, and self-esteem. When left unchecked, these issues lead to depression and eventually travel toward thoughts of suicide. Suicidal thought is often triggered by feelings of failure. For some people, feelings of failure accompany unrealistic expectations of perfection in themselves.

Satan uses failure, defeat, rejection, and guilt to begin the process of depression and suicidal thought. Depression is nothing new. An account of the depression the prophet Elijah endured is described in 1 Kings. Elijah was a great man who did much for God. Yet he suffered powerful waves of depression.

When Elijah approached the widow at Zarephath, he must have been a scary sight. Suffering from the devastating effects of depression, Elijah came out of hiding after retreating to the brook of Cherith and watching its waters slowly dry up. The widow would have been smart to leave Elijah at the town gate. Indeed, she probably had neighbors telling her she was a fool to let this prophet of doom into her home. Yet she saw Elijah's need, took him in, and ministered to him in a way that brought such a change in his perspective that a few days later he was restored to the point of healing the widow's son and blessing her household.

When Elijah asked for food, the widow said, "I don't have any bread—only a handful of flour in a jar and a little oil in a jug. I am gathering a few sticks to take home and make a meal for myself and my son, that we may eat it—and die" (1 Kings 17:12). Perhaps the widow herself had a spirit of suicide, but she quietly listened to Elijah, gave him food, and then encouraged him to see this was only a season in his life. Maybe she reminded him of the ways God had blessed his life in the past and gave him hope to believe that God would bless him in greater measure in the future. Whatever her approach, she helped Elijah make a life-saving turnaround.

Since the Bible doesn't give a full account of her life, we can only speculate. Maybe this was a chance for the widow to help in a way she had not been able to help her deceased husband. Perhaps he also suffered from depression and was a suicide victim. We'll never know for sure, but the widow saw an opportunity to make a difference in Elijah's life. Her personal plan for recovery from suicide may have been to make a difference in the lives of the depressed and suicidal whom she encountered along the way.

An account in 1 Kings 19 shows Elijah again suicidal. He went a day's journey into the wilderness and came and sat down under a broom tree. He prayed that he might die, saying, "It is enough! Now, LORD, take my life" (1 Kings 19:4 NKJV). Elijah complained to the LORD that he was alone, the only one who was zealous for God, and that people were trying to kill him.

"Then the LORD said, 'Go out and stand on the mountain in the presence of the LORD, for the LORD is about to pass by.' Then a great and powerful wind tore the mountains apart and shattered the rocks before the LORD, but the LORD was not in the wind. After the wind there was an earthquake, but the LORD was not in the earthquake. After the earthquake came a fire, but the LORD was not in the fire. And after the fire came a gentle whisper" (1 Kings 19:11–12).

God knew Elijah needed a gentle touch, a touch almost like a whisper. Elijah needed God to just brush his life. God was not in the tumultuous events in Elijah's life. He was in a whisper.

That is the answer for the depressed and suicidal today. They need God to just brush by their lives and touch them. They need a whisper from the Father. As interveners, this is all we have to offer. Apart from the Holy Spirit, we can do nothing in a hurting person's life. A list of do's and don'ts is not going to work without the brush of God in a person's life.

The saving of lives will only be accomplished by the power of the Holy Spirit working in and through people who are willing and available. It is vanity and pride to think we can save a person's life with our own skills and abilities. If it were left up to our efforts alone, no one would be saved. Skill and knowledge are tools used by God to allow us to minister more effectively to the people whom he loves. The only ability God requires is availability.

These biblical accounts show it is possible for us to be interveners. A willingness to become involved in the lives of those who are struggling is a start. The keys to preventing suicide are an understanding of what to look for and taking the necessary steps to become active in the person's life.

The goal in intervention is not just to keep the person alive but to give him something to live for. God's will for each of us is to be used in the lives of others. The choices we make are the bridge to someone else's future.

The following are clues to help you determine if someone is at increased risk for suicide from depression:

- **Change in personality**—obviously sad, withdrawn, irritable, or apathetic. A drastic improvement in personality after a person has been deeply depressed could be a red flag.
- **Depression**—extreme unhappiness and lethargy.
- **Talking about death**—an unusual preoccupation with death—asking what happens after death, buying life insurance policies, talking about writing or changing a will.
- **Direct or indirect hints at suicide**—statements about worthlessness or saying no one cares; statements like, "You're better off without me," or, "I won't be around much longer."
- **Unexplained changes in mood or behavior**—extreme sense of negativism about life in general, failure to engage in or enjoy normal activities or hobbies. A hobby like

gardening or golf, which once brought joy, is no longer of interest.

- **Changes in sleeping or eating habits**—either more or less.
- **Changes in physical appearance**—poor personal grooming; dramatic weight loss or gain; a dull, flat facial expression; fixed and glazed eyes.
- **Withdrawal and alienation**—very little communication, avoidance of friends and family members.
- **Feelings of despair**—no excitement about upcoming events, hopelessness about current circumstances or the future.
- **Increased substance abuse**—overindulgence of drugs and alcohol.
- **Anger and aggressive behavior**—quick-tempered or easily upset.
- **Fidgety, restless, ill at ease, or panicky.**
- **Giving away favorite or treasured items.**

Following are factors that may increase the likelihood that a person may be thinking about attempting suicide:

- A history of suicide in the family—statistics increase dramatically.
- A previous suicide attempt—probability increases with each attempt.
- Disability or physical illness.
- Any type of loss (relationship, job, death).
- Absence of support systems—no relationship with family or neighbors. No church affiliation.
- Inability to cope with life stresses.
- Money problems—unmanageable debt!
- Recent change in job or residence.
- A sudden improvement during or following a depression or suicidal crisis.
- Divorce—a person facing impending divorce or recently divorced and children, particularly teenagers, whose parents are divorced.

Suicide and the Elderly

Although the elderly make up only 13 percent of the population, they account for 25 percent of all suicides. Statistics show there is one suicide every eighty-three minutes for the age group over sixty-five. The suicide rate for the elderly rose 9 percent between 1980 and 1992. Lonely, isolated seniors commit many of these suicides. Minimum estimates of elder suicides range from six thousand to ten thousand annually. Often these suicides are reported as accidental deaths, especially in cases of medical overdosing.

Older adults are more lethal in their methods of suicide and have a higher completion rate. Firearms are the most common means of completing suicide among the elderly. White males over the age of 80 make up the highest risk group of all age/gender/race groups. In 1993, the suicide rate for these men was 73.6 per 100,000. A total of 81 percent of elderly suicides is male. The rate of suicide for females declines after age sixty-five.

Contrary to popular opinion, only a fraction of elderly suicide victims have been diagnosed with a terminal illness at the time of death. Two-thirds of older adults in their late sixties, seventies, and eighties are in relatively good physical health when they die by suicide. A total of 66 to 90 percent of elderly suicide victims have had at least one psychiatric diagnosis with two-thirds of these diagnoses being late-onset, single-episode clinical depression. However, depression is not a *normal* part of aging, and as many as 75 percent of depressed older Americans are at increased risk for suicide because they are not receiving treatment for depression. Older adults are less likely than younger suicidal counterparts to seek help by calling a crisis line.

How You Can Help

Be bold about confronting someone whom you suspect is suicidal. Don't be lulled into believing the myth that mentioning suicide will cause the person to attempt suicide. An individual who is depressed has probably already considered suicide and will be relieved that someone recognized his pain and his "secret is out."

Let the person know you care. As the well-known saying goes,

"People don't care what you know until they know that you care." A depressed or suicidal person will be glad you are perceptive enough to realize she is in distress. Sharing your concern for the person will help her know she is not alone in her pain.

Be a good listener. Allow a suicidal friend or family member to talk about what he is feeling. Suicidal individuals are frequently self-absorbed, inward, and noncommunicative. It is important for you to listen closely to anything the person says. Much talking on your part will not be very effective because the person is in a state of mind that will not allow him to listen or absorb all you are saying. Do everything you can to let the person know you are there for him, and willing to listen without judging or challenging.

Suggest the individual have a medical checkup. Almost always, a suicidal individual is depressed. A total of 75 percent of all suicide victims have visited their doctor within three to six months before their death. Depression often causes physical symptoms that lead people to seek medical help. Depression is treatable with medication. Offer to make an appointment for your suicidal friend or relative, and make every effort to see he keeps the appointment.

Encourage counseling. Make some calls for the person to locate a counselor or clergy. Offer to drive her to and from the appointment or baby-sit for the person so she can keep the appointment. There are even Web sites (listed below) that offer confidential e-mail counseling for individuals.

Be practical. What can you do for the person right now? Can you provide child care, meals, or transportation?

Be available. In *Hope for the Troubled Heart*, Billy Graham writes, "Being available is difficult, because it takes time, but being sensitive to the small amounts of time we can give could reap large rewards in someone's life. It doesn't really matter what we say to comfort people during a time of suffering, it's our concern and availability that count."[8]

WHEN SUICIDE HAPPENS ANYWAY

Even when you are educated, aware, and involved in suicide intervention, occasionally the person you are attempting to help will take his own life in spite of your best efforts. Realize you are fighting an uphill battle, and be realistic about the possibility that suicide may still happen. It is almost impossible to monitor a person 24/7. Don't beat yourself up if all of your efforts end up for naught. Quite frequently, if a person has made the decision to die, nothing will stop her.

During the writing of this book, I lost one of my long-time counselees to suicide. I hadn't seen Rick in months, but he showed up in my office one day in May. His physical appearance was greatly altered. I saw him leaning against the door of the counseling room as I came down the hall, and the expression on his face stopped me in my tracks. During the course of the session, I observed that he was panicky and obviously depressed. He had a lot he wanted to accomplish, but he couldn't seem to meet any of his goals. Because I felt he was suicidal, I took immediate steps to intervene. We agreed on a "no-harm contract." With this contract, the counselee promises to contact his physician, pastor, some family member, or me if he is at the brink of suicide.

I counseled Rick on a weekly basis over the next six to eight weeks, but during this time his depression seemed to worsen, in spite of continued treatment for depression by his physician. In the last session before his death, I encouraged him to again consider hospitalization, but he was resistant. I told Rick to make an appointment that day to see his doctor immediately. I called his wife as he left my office and asked her to remove all guns from the home. I put a call in to his doctor but was unable to speak with him that day. In spite of these measures, I felt Rick slipping through our fingers.

The following day I was able to talk to Rick's doctor and confirm that he had an appointment within an hour. When I finished that call, another came in. It was Rick's wife telling me he had killed himself within minutes of his scheduled doctor's appointment. He used a collectible shotgun. His wife was unaware it was even operational.

I was devastated by his death because I felt we had taken every precaution to keep it from happening. I had to deal with my anger toward him for taking his own life. The bottom line is you can't control what another person does. If a person is intent on death, he will work until he accomplishes that goal. As an intervener, you do the best you can, you pray, and if the worst happens, you recover and go on.

WHERE TO FIND HELP

American Association of Suicidology
2429 South Ash
Denver, CO 20222
1–202–237–2280
Resources for clergy, psychologists, social workers, physicians, and other professionals who are interested in suicide prevention. Distributes information through programs and publications.

International Association of Suicide Prevention
Suicide Prevention and Crisis Center
1811 Trousdale Drive
Burlingame, CA 94010
Provides information and training regarding suicide prevention.

National Committee on Youth Suicide Prevention
666 Fifth Avenue, 23d Floor
New York, NY 10103
Develops youth suicide prevention programs in local communities and provides information to increase public awareness of youth suicide.

National Save-A-Life League
44520 Fourth Avenue, Suite MH3
New York, NY 11220
An organization for professionals and trained volunteers focusing on the prevention of suicide.

The Samaritans
500 Commonwealth Avenue
Kenmore Square
Boston, MA 02215
An organization for people who volunteer their time to help the suicidal and lonely. Holds numerous talks and workshops each year on suicide prevention for professionals and lay people.

SUICIDE PREVENTION/INTERVENTION WEBSITES

American Foundation for Suicide Prevention
www.afsp.org

Centers for Disease Control and Prevention, National Center for Injury Prevention and Control
www.cdc.gov/ncipc, 404–639–3286

Institute on Aging
www.ioaging.org/programs/cesp/cesp/html
Friendship Line—1–800–971–0016 (24-hour counseling)

National Strategy for Suicide Prevention
www.mentalhealth.org/suicideprevention/

The Jason Foundation, Inc.
1–888–881–2323, **www.jasonfoundation.com**

www.metanoia.org/sucide
Conversations and writings for the suicidal to read. If you are feeling suicidal, be sure to read this page before you take any action. It could save your life.

The National Hopeline Network
1–800-SUICIDE (1–800–784–2433)
www.hopeline.com

National Institute of Mental Health
Treatment for Adolescents with Depression Study (TADS)—
www.nimh.nih.gov/studies/tads.cfm

National Mental Health Awareness Campaign
www.nostigma.org
For local referrals, and crisis intervention, call 1–877–495–0009

The Samaritans—www.befrienders.org/suicide.htm

SAVE—Suicide Awareness Voices of Education
www.save.org, E-mail: save@winternet.com

Suicide Information and Education Centre www.suicideinfo.ca/siec

Suicide Prevention Training
QPR (Question, Persuade, Refer) Institute www.qprinstitute.com

Yellow Ribbon Suicide Prevention Program www.yellowribbon.org

Youth Suicide Prevention Programs: A Resource Guide
www.cdc.gov/ncipc/pub-res/youthsui.htm

CHAPTER 8

⚬

Restoration:
Double Joy

"He has sent me to bind up the brokenhearted, . . . to comfort all who mourn, and provide for those who grieve, . . . to bestow on them a crown of beauty instead of ashes, the oil of gladness instead of mourning, and a garment of praise instead of a spirit of despair. . . . They will rebuild the ancient ruins and restore the places long devastated; they will renew the ruined cities that have been devastated for generations. . . . Instead of their shame my people will receive a double portion, and instead of disgrace they will rejoice in their inheritance; and so they will inherit a double portion in their land, and everlasting joy will be theirs" (Isa. 61:1–4, 7).

*T*here has been much discussion regarding whether to rebuild the twin towers of the World Trade Center in New York following their destruction on September 11, 2001. One school of thought holds the towers should be rebuilt higher and more spectacular than before as a reminder of the strength and resilience of the American spirit. The other line of thinking suggests leaving the spot barren of structures except for a memorial to those who lost their lives in the attack. Already architectural renderings of both the new towers and a memorial park have been unveiled. As of the writing of this book, no decision has been reached on which plan to follow.

In the yearlong process of cleaning up the World Trade Center site, tons of ashes and debris were removed from the location by truck and barge. The clean-up process was grueling but necessary before any type of restoration of the site could even be considered.

As a suicide survivor, you are faced with a similar decision. You can either take on the tedious task of clearing the debris from your ground zero and do the necessary site work to lay a new foundation, or you can build a shrine to your grief and live the rest of your life in an unrestored state.

In her book, *Just Enough Light for the Step I'm On— Trusting God in the Tough Times,* Stormie Omartian says,
When tragedy happens, it's normal to feel that life has come to a complete standstill. But actually it's life as you *knew* it that has stopped. Your new life, *without* that which was lost, is going forward. You just can't see it yet. Even though it's hard to imagine the future being any different than it is at that moment, healing and restoration are happening. You won't always feel this way. There *will* be an end. The loss may have been sudden, but the transition to your new life must be traveled one step at a time. . . . Even if your well of tears seems to never run dry, continue to walk in the light of God's presence and you *will* make it through the river of grief to the other side. If you can't see ahead, it's okay. God will not only provide enough light for your next step, he will also enable you to take it.[9]

Following is the story of the decision one survivor made to go on with life and the steps she took to reach joy.

CELEBRATING VICTORY

On a day that would plunge others back into the depths of grief, Jeanne and Mike celebrated. They commemorated the one-year anniversary of Patrick's living in heaven.

On August 21, 2001, Jeanne and Mike's twenty-three-year-old son, Patrick, killed himself. For years he struggled with severe ADD and depression. Although he used alcohol and drugs as a teenager, he had been clean and sober for six years. He was instrumental in helping others overcome substance abuse as well. Patrick left his parents a tape on which he recorded his prayer asking God to forgive him for taking his own life.

"We were told we would *never* get over this," Jeanne and Mike say. "But people simply do not understand the power of the Lord to heal and his victory over death. This doesn't mean that it isn't incredibly painful, but God's Word says that our Shepherd walks us *through* the valley; no need to live there forever. We all have losses in life, and when we push the pain down and try to mourn quickly, we delay healing instead. Healing is a slow, step-by-step process. Don't try to rush through it.

"At some point I realized I'd been dragging around a load of ashes since Patrick's death. I grieved that he missed his destiny. I cried a lot, deep sobbing cries. I was very angry. I spoke my rage. It hurt me physically to mourn. My stomach hurt, literally. Then I read in Isaiah 61 that the God of all comfort is willing to make an exchange. So I made the decision to dump my truckloads of ashes at his doorstep, every ash a seed for beauty. God poured his healing oil into me and has shown me how to exchange the ashes for his beauty. In my sorrow, the Lord has given me joy. I've exchanged other life hurts, too. I do this daily by writing down the hurt, pronouncing forgiveness, and saying these are ashes, I give them to you in exchange for your beauty.

"Also, as part of my healing, I write letters to others I know who have encountered suicide in their lives. I know there are many others because at Patrick's funeral, I encountered at least nine other people who struggled with issues relating to suicide. As I encourage others, I heal in the process. I tell others to focus on things that make them happy instead of their sorrow. Survivors need a message that is encouraging and hopeful."

ॐ ॐ ॐ

OVERCOMING FEAR WITH FAITH
"For God has not given us a spirit of fear, but a spirit of power and of love and of a sound mind" (2 Tim. 1:7 NKJV).

Fear is probably the greatest deterrent to living a life of restoration and joy for anyone, suicide survivor or not. As one of the most prevalent aftermaths of suicide, fear is something that must be confronted. Following suicide, a variety of fears come into play—fear of the unknown, fears regarding the loss of material possessions, a potential move, fears about lifestyle changes, strained relationships, and financial concerns. Along with these fears come the more intangible fears of feeling violated and vulnerable. To some extent, fear may be a continual struggle for suicide survivors even years later.

As a suicide survivor, you must avoid sinking into a trap of anxiety and fear and following the same path as your loved one. Fear is one of life's primary emotions. It is probably the underlying emotion that caused your loved one to end his life. Usually, for a man, the fear of failure is the most overwhelming. If he has health problems, he begins to fear he will lose his job. Looming financial obligations—a mortgage, an uninsured surgery, or college tuition—all are sources of fear. *What if I lose my job? How am I going to provide for my family?*

Sometimes just seeing a friend or neighbor with seemingly "more" who is better able to provide for his family can lead a man down a winding path toward low self-esteem and feelings of failure. At the root of it all is fear: *I can't give my children what they want and need. I'm a bad parent.* These kinds of thoughts stem from fear, but they lead rapidly to anger. *It's not fair. Why should they have all the luck?* This anger, when unresolved, becomes depression, and untreated depression often leads to suicide.

Fear is almost always irrational. Even now, years after my father's suicide, I am occasionally overcome with a sense of panic when I'm alone in the car. Suddenly, I start thinking, *What if I fail? What happens if my clients suddenly stop making appointments? What happens if my business fails? I have a wife, five children, and a dog! How will I take care of them?* Although I know this fear is ridiculous because I have been in a private counseling practice for over ten years, I still deal with the fear.

Often being afraid becomes a source of fear itself. *What's wrong with me? Why am I so afraid?* The irrational part also comes in when we are afraid to name the fear and confront it. We feel if it remains unnamed it is under control.

Following my father's death, fear was my constant companion, but I never mentioned it. I felt as if I existed under a black cloud. There was something unsettling and disturbing about the fact that my father was so profoundly unhappy that he chose to kill himself. I had fears that I would kill myself too because of a darkness or hidden quality about my father that I never recognized which must also exist in me.

In the back of my mind was anxiety that my mother was also going to die. My fear was not that she would commit suicide because my only experience with suicide involved a man. My father killed himself, so I reasoned only men killed themselves. The fear regarding losing my mother was that she would succumb to cancer. When both of my sisters were involved in separate auto accidents within months following my father's death, I felt incredibly vulnerable and unable to control the world around me.

On the day my Sunday school teacher told me of my father's death, she handed me a slip of paper. On it was Psalm 56:3: "When I am afraid, I will trust in you." That short little verse was revolutionary for me. It was the first time I can remember God's Word speaking to me. This verse let me know it was *normal* for me to feel frightened because the verse says "when." Every suicide survivor is looking for a way to feel normal again following a life event that is so abnormal. I encourage you to find passages in the Bible that give you comfort and speak directly to you and your situation.

The words "fear not" are mentioned at least 240 times in the Bible. God knows that as humans we will struggle with fear. So he instructs us over and over in his Word not to fear. Isaiah 41:10 reminds us, "So do not fear, for I am with you; do not be dismayed, for I am your God. I will strengthen you and help you; I will uphold you with my righteous right hand."

Fear is a part of being human, something everyone battles at one time or another, but we don't have to *remain* in fear. Often God allows fear in order to point us toward him instead of continuing to focus on the problem or event. Second Timothy 1:7 tells us God did not give us a spirit of fear. If fear is not from God, where does it come from? Satan is the source. He tricks us into believing that worry is an effective weapon against fear. John 8:44 refers to Satan as the "father of lies." If fear is from Satan, it is a lie.

I once counseled a woman who believed if she worried enough about a situation, it would not happen. Satan tricked her into believing an appropriate way to control future events in her life was to worry about them to an extreme degree. Then the dreaded things would not occur. This mind-set is superstitious in nature and in direct opposition to God's Word. Many times we are fearful because we do not know or understand the Word. Fear is the result of judging reality on the basis of what we are experiencing rather than on who God is.

Satan uses the same deception today that he used with Eve. Satan asked, "Did God really say that?" (see Gen. 3:1). He tempted her by challenging God's authority and causing her to believe God was withholding something she deserved. Satan used similar arguments with Jesus in the wilderness by quoting Old Testament Scripture. Jesus responded with Scripture, and this is also an appropriate way for us to combat fear. Having a ready arsenal of verses memorized and available to quote helps defeat Satan's battle plan of fear.

Fear robs God of his power and authority. If you believe God can't, then what you desire will not happen. Mark 6:5–6 records that Jesus was unable to do any miracles among the people, and he was amazed by their lack of faith. Faith is the opposite of fear. In fact, fear is faith that something bad will happen. Instead, God moves where there is faith in him, where he is pleased and welcome. Hebrews 11:1 gives this definition of faith: "Now faith is being sure of what we hope for and certain of what we do not see." The eleventh chapter of Hebrews provides a roll call of Bible characters who lived by faith. The benefit for those who live by faith is God's blessing and peace.

Following are steps to overcoming fear by replacing it with faith:

1. **Repent.** Upon first seeing this word, most people think about repentance from sin because repentance usually is equated with turning from sin. But in this situation, *repent* does not imply sinful behavior nor connect your loved one's suicide to you or your behavior. *Repent* in this instance is in regard to mind-set. The Greek phrase for *repent* is

metanoia, which means a change of mind or a change of direction. As a suicide survivor, you have to choose actively to change what you believe. In this case, the choice is to turn from fear and embrace faith.

Suicide is like a yawning crater in your life. Often when a crater forms during an earthquake, it sucks everything in around it. Sometimes after dragging objects in, it abruptly closes. As a suicide survivor, you are also in danger of being pulled in. You need to head rapidly in the other direction both spiritually and emotionally by basing reality on God's truth rather than feelings of fear born from Satan's lies regarding suicide.

Acts 3:19 in the Amplified Bible says, "So repent (change your mind and purpose); turn around and return [to God], that your sins may be erased (blotted out, wiped clean), that times of refreshing (of recovering from the effects of heat, of reviving with fresh air) may come from the presence of the Lord."

Many times an emotional upheaval such as suicide in a person's life will cause him to reevaluate his life's purpose and spiritual connection. Following the initial crisis of suicide, you may experience a renewed sense of wanting to be right with God, live a life pleasing to him, and experience his presence in a new way. This can be accomplished by changing your direction toward a deeper faith in God. You will be renewed and refreshed by the decision to move closer to God and change your direction regarding living a life of fear following suicide.

2. **Discipline words and thoughts.** Along with choosing to think differently comes taking every thought captive and renewing your mind. It may be helpful to view the mind as an air traffic controller. Your thoughts are like circling airplanes. Numerous thoughts are waiting to land on the runway of your mind. Some thoughts are excellent, edifying, and worthy of a landing lane on the runway. Others are thoughts created by looking at circumstances. They are fearful and discouraging like a rickety, unsafe airplane.

As the air traffic controller, your mind can choose to permit thought-planes to land. If your thought-tower allows negative, self-defeating thoughts to land, taxi, reach the gate, and deplane, those thoughts infiltrate and contaminate your heart and mind, just as deplaning passengers disperse in a busy airport. It would be impossible to reassemble those passengers and remove them from the airport; so it is difficult to gather and reject negative thoughts once they develop into a mental pattern. Decide now to wave those thoughts away from the runway of your mind.

Mind renewal is a journey following repentance. Renewal is not a one-time event. It is a continuous process. Second Corinthians 10:5 encourages taking captive every thought to make it obedient to Christ. Romans 12:2 says, "Do not conform any longer to the pattern of this world, but be transformed by the renewing of your mind."

Renew your mind and redirect negative thought patterns through study of God's Word. Listen to what you are saying and what Scripture says. Are the two in agreement? Are you speaking blessings or curses? Our words are either words of blessing or cursing; there is no third choice. Deuteronomy 30:19–20 says, "I have set before you life and death, blessings and curses. Now choose life, so that you and your children may live and that you may love the LORD your God, listen to his voice, and hold fast to him. For the LORD is your life."

Life is a multiple-choice test, and God gives us the right answer—LIFE. In order for you and your descendants to live, you *must* choose life. God doesn't decide for you. You must make the choice to break the pattern of death and curse by choosing life.

Are your thought patterns and conversations faith-driven or fear-driven? Philippians 4:8 reminds us to think about things that are true, noble, right, pure, lovely, admirable, excellent, and praiseworthy.

If you want to know if you are living in fear, listen to what you are saying. If you hear worry and doubt in your words, you are not living in the truth of God's Word. Words shape attitudes. You cannot "feel" your way into a right action, but you can always act or behave your way into the feeling. "The good man brings good things out of the good stored up in his heart. . . . For out of the overflow of his heart his mouth speaks" (Luke 6:45).

3. **Relinquish your fears to God.** Give God all your cares. First Peter 5:7 instructs us to "cast all your anxiety on him because he cares for you." It is futile to worry about something God is taking care of.

Philippians 4:6–7 tell us not to worry and offers added promise of peace. Trust God. Look for ways God is working things out for your good. Visualize and speak the answers to your fears in prayer instead of telling God the impossibility of your circumstances. Watch in faith as God resolves situations that seem unsolvable, and live in peace.

4. **Use your faith.** Trust the power of the Holy Spirit within to help you make a conscious choice to break the cycle of suicide.

- Suicide has a tremendously isolating effect. Make sure you talk about your feelings, particularly with family members.
- Separate the way the person died from the rest of his life. Remember positive points about the person.
- Employ self-talk. Say, *I'm not like that.* Tell yourself why you are not going to repeat the family history of suicide. Remind yourself of all the good things about your life.
- Strike a balance between appropriate grieving and living in a continual spirit of grief and fear. Yes, grieve for your loved one. Then take steps to move on with your life. You are not dishonoring your loved one by getting on with life. Live with the message of hope in 1 Thessalonians 4:13–14, "Brothers, we do not want you to be ignorant about those who fall asleep, or to grieve like the rest of men, who have no hope. We believe that Jesus died and rose again and so we believe that God will bring with Jesus those who have fallen asleep in him."
- Have a list of people you are going to contact who will talk you out of suicide if you feel yourself slipping into that thought pattern. Decide you will never consider suicide without first telling someone the direction of your thoughts.
- Call a family meeting and covenant together never to follow the suicide path. Ask your pastor to be present as a witness to your family pledge.
- Remind yourself daily of ways you see God's provision and blessing in your life in spite of the devastation of suicide.
- Choose to live life fully and victoriously.

WHY COUNSELING?
"Where there is no counsel, the people fall; but in the multitude of counselors there is safety" (Prov. 11:14 NKJV).

The reaction, grieving, coping, and healing process is unique for each person. The stages of grieving, which usually follow the *sad, mad, glad* pattern, may be complicated with other factors such as embarrassment—what the death says about your family member, what the death says about you, rejection, and fear of abandonment. Suicide survivors have feelings of guilt to go along with the grieving process.

If you feel you are experiencing a prolonged stay in any one of these stages, you may need help to move beyond it. The following survey will help you determine if you or a loved one should consider seeing a counselor.

EVALUATION
Check the following statements that apply:

_____ I cannot function for days at a time because of my grief.

_____ Since my loved one's suicide, I feel unbearable pain that I'm worried will never end.

_____ I feel I should have done more to prevent this suicide.

_____ I have recurring, troubling dreams about my lost loved one.

_____ I cry all the time while thinking about my loved one and the way he or she died.

_____ I am angry with God because he could have prevented this and didn't.

_____ I find myself living in a fantasy world where the suicide didn't really happen.

_____ I feel others should share the blame for my loved one's suicide.

_____ I think this suicide is God's punishment for something I have done.

_____ If the pain doesn't get any better, I will probably kill myself too.

_____ I find myself relying on drugs or alcohol to cope with the pain.

_____ I feel that the future is hopeless, and I have no reason to go on living.

If you checked three or more items on this list, you should consider going to professional counseling.

What to Expect: The Counseling Process

For many people counseling is a last resort. Some view the need for counseling as a personal failure. They feel they should be able to cope with the emotional trauma on their own. I wish that was not the case because the longer a person suppresses his emotions, the harder it is to process them later.

People vary greatly in the speed with which they move through counseling. Even though all want to feel better, most are reluctant to pull up the pain with which they are trying to cope. Sometimes well-meaning people want survivors to have a doctor prescribe medication to deal with the emotional pain. I discourage this unless the individual can't function at all or can't sleep. My experience has been that family members don't want to see a loved one upset, but anesthetizing the pain will slow the healing process.

Individuals can expect it to be difficult to submit to the counseling process. Many procrastinate, dealing with estate issues or other things that appear to need attention over emotional issues. Three to six months after the death is a good time to think about going for help. Earlier than that, shock is still a factor, and counseling may not be as effective.

Shock is a medical term that describes the body's reaction to danger. Most people equate shock with emotional trauma, but it really refers to physical levels that are out of norm. Shock is a protection mechanism that the body has for coping with overload. A person may be in pain but not remember it later. Our minds have a "breaker box" to deal with emotional pain; the emotional system shuts down. After a suicide the mind won't let you feel the full extent of the emotional pain until some time has passed. People usually come to counseling when the mind will let them believe it is safe to do it, and they realize it won't kill them to face the pain.

Counseling will probably precipitate some dreams and flashbacks that are disturbing and emotionally painful. Many people decide that they don't want to go through this. With other types of counseling, I can give people a game plan, some active steps to improve the situation. Suicide survivor counseling is different. Some people feel much better talking about their pain. Within a few sessions they are able to move on. This is certainly not the case with everyone.

Just as a cut on your hand heals, so the emotional cut heals from talking about the pain. You may be physically exhausted after a counseling session because it is very hard work emotionally.

In the first counseling session, my goal is to establish rapport with the counselee. When appropriate, I always reveal that I am a suicide survivor. I ask the counselee to take me back to the day of the suicide and tell me every detail he can remember. I encourage recounting the funeral and the counselee's feelings on that day. I initiate discussion of eternity and verify the survivor's own relationship to Jesus Christ. It is also helpful to gather some genealogy to see if there are family patterns. I listen to understand what the person is saying as well as listen for a personal level of depression and suicidality. I then establish a verbal no-harm contract in which the counselee promises to call me at any time if he feels suicidal himself. At the end of the session, I usually suggest some reading for the counselee.

In the second session I address the issues of anger, guilt, shame, and bewilderment. It may take several sessions to deal with these issues. If it has been a while since the suicide, I ask the counselee to name life events, such as weddings, births, etc., that the person missed. If it has been years since the suicide, I encourage the counselee to visualize what the loved one would look like or what that person's life would be like today.

Another exercise that is helpful is to get family members together and compare puzzle pieces. Comparing notes and talking about the events surrounding the suicide with family members helps fill in the blanks. It is especially good to bring up pleasant characteristics and memories of the deceased so you avoid remembering the person only by the way in which he or she died. It is good to actually practice saying the word *suicide*. Avoidance of saying the word also brings hesitancy to talk about the circumstances of the death.

In subsequent sessions I have counselees write a letter to the deceased loved one. I encourage them to say everything they want to the person. I especially suggest they tell the deceased how hard life is for the survivor and vent the anger. I compare this to a good "emotional vomit." Just as a person who has a stomachache feels better after throwing up, so the counselee is able to tie up loose ends regarding anger toward the deceased with a letter. Once the letter is written and everything has been said, the letter needs to be destroyed.

I also encourage support group attendance and regular church involvement. The goal in counseling is for the suicide survivor to get to the point where talking about the suicide doesn't bring on searing pain or a total emotional meltdown. There will always be a scar. As with a physical scar, the memory of what caused the wound will always be vivid. There is remembrance of how much the wound hurt at the time it happened, but the actual pain is not relived. The scar is still visible, but the debilitating emotional pain is gone.

Sometimes a counselee gets stuck on an issue and can't move beyond it. When this happens, I ask the person to think what she is telling herself. Usually, the issue involved is unforgiveness. I try to help the person see that not forgiving leads to bitterness, and this blots out all chance of recovery. The counselee must make a quality decision to forgive and then actually do it. Forgiveness is not a feeling. It is a powerful transaction that does not require the offending person's cooperation in order to take place. Many people use noncooperation or unavailability as an excuse not to forgive.

Forgiveness can take place between you and God alone. You do have control over the situation. When you can consistently tell yourself as you think of that person, "God bless you, I forgive you, I love you," then you know you are forgiving. Only then can you expect the feeling of forgiveness to come. Forgiveness is an ongoing process.

The Freedom of Forgiveness

Forgiveness is the central tenant of our Christian faith, but it is a concept that many of us find difficult to grasp and execute in everyday life. Why is it so hard to extend the gift of forgiveness?

Although it takes effort to forgive, the benefits of forgiveness are attainable. Whether the product of pride, indifference, or fear, unforgiveness ruins relationships, breeds anger, and renders happiness illusive. Often the inability to forgive weighs on our souls, clouding the past and dimming the present.

Unforgiveness is the root of many of the problems I see in my counseling ministry. I counsel people who are hurting, disappointed, and bitter but can't bring themselves to the point of forgiving. So many people do not understand forgiveness in biblical terms. They fail to see that it is to their benefit to forgive. Unforgiveness blocks relationships with God and others. Not only does it affect mental health; it affects physical health in the form of high blood pressure and strokes.

There are a number of misconceptions about forgiveness:

If I forgive, it makes me look weak. Many people have the mistaken idea that if they forgive it is a sign of weakness. Luke 23:33–34 tells us that Jesus forgave even in his hour of greatest physical weakness while on the cross. He forgave while those around him were unrepentant. He took the complete responsibility of forgiveness. In the world's eyes this seems like weakness. But Jesus was not weak. He showed the greatest strength imaginable by forgiving those who mocked him.

By forgiving, I give up control. Actually, there is less control in unforgiveness because you give the offending person control over your emotions. Mark 11: 25 instructs us to forgive anyone we have something against so that the Father in heaven may forgive us. Living in a state of unforgiveness causes us to lose our right standing with God. To ensure a relationship with God, you must forgive others as God has forgiven you.

I may get hurt again if I forgive. There's always that chance, but forgiveness is worth the risk because it brings immediate relief. In forgiving, we lay down a heavy burden. A splinter analogy helps counselees get past this roadblock to forgiveness. When you have a splinter, there is pain and discomfort. In order to feel better, you must remove the splinter. It's going to hurt, maybe even more for a short time while you dig it out. But in order to remove it, you have to

endure some additional pain. Once the splinter is out, there is immediate relief. Forgiveness is the same way. The process may cause some
additional pain, but once done, the relief is immediate.

The offender needs to pay for what he did. Isaiah 53:5 reminds
us that Jesus took the punishment. The payment has already been
made. Not forgiving implies Jesus' atonement is not enough or that
certain people need additional punishment.

If I ignore the pain, it will go away. Not only will the pain not
disappear; it will eventually turn to bitterness. Bitterness is nothing
more than stagnant anger. Depression is the result of unresolved
anger, and our world is full of depressed people. Hebrews 12:15
addresses bitterness: "See to it that no one misses the grace of God
and that no bitter root grows up to cause trouble and defile many."

I'll do it later—waiting for a better time. Ephesians 4:26 tells us
not to let the sun go down on our anger. There is no better time than
now. Forgiveness should be done quickly. Scripture reminds us that
God's time is always *right now.* When you let the sun go down on
your anger, you've given the devil a foothold.

It will be too emotionally painful to stir up old feelings. Yes,
there will be emotional pain, but you have to deal with the pain in
order to heal and move on. Stirred-up feelings are God's stop sign
saying you need to confront the pain and deal with it.

Forgiveness seems too easy. Many feel merely saying, "I forgive,"
is too simple. Forgiveness doesn't require a complicated set of rules
or steps. By divine design, forgiveness involves humility and grace.

More often than not, forgiveness is an act of the will rather than
a feeling. Romans 10:9–10 says, "If you confess with your mouth,
'Jesus is Lord,' and believe in your heart that God raised him from the
dead, you will be saved. For it is with your heart that you believe and
are justified, and it is with your mouth that you confess and are saved."

Two things are required in this passage: confessing and believing. It
is interesting that the confessing comes before the believing. Similarly,
the act of speaking forgiveness usually comes before the feeling of forgiveness. Realize that you are not the only person who hurts in a broken
relationship, and choose to forgive whether you feel like it or not.

Forgiveness is not forgetting; it is remembering without the pain. Neither is forgiveness excusing or tolerating. True forgiveness occurs when a person decides to extend the gift of forgiveness by letting someone "off the hook" for an offense. Forgiveness is about giving up your right to hurt someone because you have been hurt. In making the quality decision to forgive, you discover the path to freedom and peace.

Probably the most difficult decision a suicide survivor faces is the choice of forgiveness. The concept of forgiving someone who is dead may seem strange. But because the loved one is gone, it is all the more essential for the survivor to forgive. God is a forgiving God. He sent Jesus to bear the penalty for our sins so we could be forgiven. If we follow God's example, we must also forgive.

For those who blame God for suicide, it is important for survivors to understand the difference between causing and allowing. God never causes a suicide, but he does allow it. This brings us again to freedom of choice. God gives us free will; therefore, those who commit suicide have freely taken that path.

Forgiving others you may be blaming for your loved one's death is another necessary area of forgiveness. It is easy to fall into the trap of blaming. Let it go. Realize your loved one made the choice to die. Forgive your loved one for making a bad decision, and then stop blaming others for his death. Continual blaming causes you to stagnate in the grieving process. The reality is that your loved one chose to die. Make the decision to forgive, heal, and get on with your life.

My ultimate goal is to help counselees see that God works things together for their good. He is able to use even the pain of suicide to bring about something good in their lives.

FIVE PRACTICAL STEPS TO FORGIVENESS

1. Write down the offense, using as much detail as possible. As you write, you may discover a level of intensity you were previously unaware of. The process of writing is a way to transfer the hurt from your heart to the paper. This transfer helps you look at the offense

more objectively and allows cleansing to occur. The more specific the description, the more complete the forgiveness.

2. Tell God out loud that you release the offender from the offense. (It is not necessary to go to the offender and voice this because the person may be unaware of your hurt or the person may be deceased.) Then bless aloud the person who offended you. By doing this you are returning good for evil as commanded in Romans 12:21. Choosing not to do this blocks us from receiving God's forgiveness for our sins. "For if you forgive men when they sin against you, your heavenly Father will also forgive you. But if you do not forgive men their sins, your Father will not forgive your sins" (Matt. 6:14–15).

3. If you need forgiveness for something you've said or done, go to the person you've offended and ask for forgiveness. Even if the person refuses to forgive, you have done your part toward reconciliation. This will mean a great deal to you in the future.

4. Let go of self-condemnation; forgive yourself. For some people, self-forgiveness is the hardest. Nothing is accomplished by living the rest of your life in an attitude of continual grief and self-punishment. Make the decision to move forward. We are promised that following confession, God casts our sin as far as the east is from the west and remembers it no more. Claim this promise and live life victoriously.

5. Destroy the written account as an act of closure.

Choosing Joy

Most people experience events in their lives that could be considered devastating life crises. Whether you are a "victor over" or a "victim of" these events is not based on the magnitude of the crises but rather on your attitude. Failure to bring closure to these events drains you of energy better spent in other pursuits. Pouring all your energies into something you can't change saps you of resources you need to live life to its fullest in the present.

Suicide survivors have a tendency to avoid ever having a good time again, thinking they are honoring the deceased. Please don't adopt this philosophy. Give yourself permission to have fun! Do the things you enjoyed doing with your loved one. He or she would want you to continue with your life.

We began this book with Joseph's words in Genesis 50:20—an act meant for evil that God used for good. Much like an earthquake, suicide is a devastating event. Over time you rebuild. You've met people in the book who are surviving. The void is still there, but God is able to bring about good.

But the story doesn't end with Genesis 50:20. Verse 21 says, "'So then, don't be afraid. I will provide for you and your children.' And he reassured them and spoke kindly to them." God reminds us not to be afraid. After tragedy, that is the most prevalent emotion. God offers the promise of provision for you and those whom you love. Joseph's love for his family is a picture of God's love for us. God wants to comfort you and speak kindly to you. Then you in turn should offer comfort to others. Second Corinthians 1:3–4 says, "Praise be to the God and Father of our Lord Jesus Christ, the Father of compassion and the God of all comfort, who comforts us in all our troubles, so that we can comfort those in any trouble with the comfort we ourselves have received from God."

God wants to bless you and give you joy. Satan works hard to rob you of that joy by using suicide to perpetuate a lifetime of fear, anger, and ineffectiveness. By continuing to make the physical act of suicide a focal point, you are choosing spiritual and emotional suicide. You also predispose future generations to a like mind-set.

I have a good life because I choose to view it as such. I believe I have a double portion of joy. God has blessed me in spite of my father's suicide. God can use me in ways he doesn't use other people because of what I have experienced. The opportunities I have to counsel suicide survivors and others through the counseling room and to host a radio call-in counseling program are a result of God's faithfulness. God has used and continues to use the earthquake of suicide in my life in ways that touch other people's lives for good. To me that is the ultimate in overcoming.

One of my greatest sources of joy is being a present, active father to my children. My relationship with my father was cut short. In being there for my children, I heal the wound my father's absence created in my life. Allow God the authority to remove the ash heap of suicide from your life—and then give him credit for doing so. Then look for your sources of joy and claim them. Live in victory.

AFTERGLOW

Consider taking a half-day or full-day retreat to the mountains or lake alone. Pray and ask yourself the following questions:

1. Am I living in faith or in fear?

2. Have I allowed myself to settle into a spirit of grief for my loved one that is dragging me under emotionally and spiritually?

3. Would my loved one feel sad that I am living in continual grief, or would he or she want me to move on with my life?

4. Am I setting an example of fear and grief for my children and grandchildren?

5. Make a list of your greatest fears.

6. Now write a letter to God or pray aloud. Confess and relinquish your fears, spirit of grief, and negative thoughts.

7. Spend time reading God's Word. Look up the passages mentioned in this chapter and copy them on note cards that you can carry with you or place throughout your home. Meditate on God's Word and begin the journey of renewing your mind.

8. Pray about persons to whom you need to extend the gift of forgiveness. List their names, and take steps to restore any broken relationships. If the person you need to forgive is dead, write a note you wish that person could read.

9. List your sources of joy and give thanks.

SUGGESTED READING

Les Carter and Frank Minirth. *The Choosing to Forgive Workbook.* Nashville, TN: Thomas Nelson Publishers, 2000. A workbook format that helps you personalize a plan to truly forgive those who have wronged you.

Charles Stanley. *The Gift of Forgiveness.* Nashville, TN: Thomas Nelson Publishers, 1987,1991. Offers specifics on how to make forgiveness an on-going, practical experience in your life.

Stormie Omartian. *Just Enough Light for the Step I'm On: Trusting God in the Tough Times.* Eugene, OR: Harvest House, 1999. Encouragement for those enduring the sadness, loneliness, and emptiness of loss.

Harold Ivan Smith. *A Decembered Grief: Living with Loss While Others Are Celebrating.* Kansas City, MO: Beacon Hill Press of Kansas City, 1999. Offers short selections to help grievers cope with holidays and anniversaries.

Joyce Meyer. *Battlefield of the Mind.* New York: Warner Faith, 1995. For those struggling with worry, anger, doubt, depression, confusion, and condemnation. Find out how to recognize dangerous thought patterns and stop them from influencing your life.

Tim LaHaye and Bob Phillips, *Anger Is a Choice.* Grand Rapids: Zondervan, 1982. 2002. Help to understand anger and directions on how to control it.

Granger Westberg, *Good Grief: A Constructive Approach to the Problem of Loss.* Minneapolis: Fortress Press, 1962, 1971, 1999. A short, easy-to-read book to help you learn what happens as you experience grief and how to move beyond your loss to "good" grief.

Charles Stanley, *How to Handle Adversity.* Nashville: Thomas Nelson Publishers, 1989. Wisdom and practical advice on how to respond to hard times.

James Dobson, *When God Doesn't Make Sense.* Wheaton, IL: Tyndale House Publishers, Inc., 1993. Everyone experiences difficulties that are not easy to understand. This book offers insights into coping with the trials of life.

French O'Shields, *Slaying the Giant: Practical Help for Understanding Preventing & Overcoming Depression.* Surfside Beach, SC: Hem of His Garment, 1994. For those who personally have depression or have a friend or love one who struggles with depression.

Endnotes

CHAPTER 3

1. Diane Hales and Robert E. Hales, "When a Teenager Is Sad . . . Pay Attention!" *Parade, The Sunday Magazine,* 5 May 2002, 4.

2. *Report of the Secretary's Task Force on Youth Suicide* (Washington, D.C.: U.S. Government Printing Office, 1989, Vol. 3, DHHS Publication No. ADM 89–1623), 3–110. www.youth.org/loco/PERSONProject/Resources/ResearchStudies/suicide.html.

3. John Leo, "Could Suicide Be Contagious?" *Time,* 24 February, 1986, 59.

4. Sandra Hughes, "Unhappy in Utah" (Logan, Utah: *CBS News,* 3 June 2002). www.cbsnes.com/stories/2002/06/03/eveningnews/printable510918.shtml.

5. Harold C. Warlick Jr., *The Rarest of These Is Hope: Christians Facing Difficult Times* (Lima, Ohio: CSS Publishing Company, 1985), 126–27.

CHAPTER 6

6. John H. Hewitt, *After Suicide* (Philadelphia: Westminster Press, 1980), 44–45.

7. Randy Christian, "After a Suicide: What is the best way to serve those left behind?" (ChristianityToday.com, Leadership Journal, Pastoral Care, Fall 1997). www.christianitytoday.com/le/714/714084.html.

CHAPTER 7

8. Billy Graham, *Hope for the Troubled Heart* (Dallas: Word Publishing, 1991), 183.

CHAPTER 8

9. Stormie Omartian, *Just Enough Light for the Step I'm On—Trusting God in the Tough Times* (Eugene, Oreg.: Harvest House Publishers, 1999), 155.